Berlitz®

Indo

phrase book & di...

Berlitz Publishing
New York   London   Singapore

Contacting the Editors
Every effort has been made to provide accurate information in this publication, but changes are inevitable. The publisher cannot be responsible for any resulting loss, inconvenience or injury. We would appreciate it if readers would call our attention to any errors or outdated information. We also welcome your suggestions; if you come across a relevant expression not in our phrase book, please contact us at: **comments@berlitzpublishing.com**

All Rights Reserved
© 2007 Berlitz Publishing/APA Publications (UK) Ltd.
Berlitz Trademark Reg. U.S. Patent Office and other countries. Marca Registrada. Used under license from Berlitz Investment Corporation.

Eleventh Printing: June 2012
Printed in China

Publishing Director: Mina Patria
Commissioning Editor: Kate Drynan
Editorial Assistant: Sophie Cooper
Translation: updated by Wordbank
Cover Design: Beverley Speight
Interior Design: Beverley Speight
Production Manager: Raj Trivedi
Picture Researcher: Beverley Speight
Cover Photo: All photos Corrie Wingate/APA except 'currency' photo iStockphoto.

Interior Photos: All photography Corrie Wingate/APA except Alex Havret 43; Ming Tang Evans/APA 56; Greg Gladman 121; James Macdonald/APA 176; Britta Jaschinski/APA 46; Mina Patria 24; Beverley Speight 53; iStockphoto 15,18, 36,39, 48, 59, 150, 151, 154, 156, 158, 160, 163.

Contents

Survival

Contents

Food & Drink

People

Leisure Time

Special Requirements

In an Emergency

Dictionary

Pronunciation

This section is designed to make you familiar with the sounds of the Indonesian language using our simplified phonetic transcription. You'll find the pronunciation of the letters and sounds in Indonesian explained below, together with their 'imitated' equivalents. This system is used throughout the phrase book; simply read the pronunciation as if it were English, noting any special rules below.

Vowels

The pronunciation of some Indonesian vowels is slightly different to English ones.

Letter	Symbol Used	Approximate Pronunciation	Example	Phonetic transcription
a	ah	a as in spa	**apa**	*ah·pah*
e	eh	e as in bed, enter, resume	**emper**	*ehm·pehr*
e	ə	a as in about, sofa	**empat, terbang**	*əm·paht, tər·bahng*
i	ee	ee as in eerie, free	**ini**	*ee·nee*
i	i	i as in sing, miss, pin	**dingin**	*dee·ngin*
o	oh	o as in only	**obat**	*oh·baht*
u	oo	oo as in book	**buku**	*boo·koo*
ai	ai	as in eye, bye	**cukai**	*choo·kai*
au	ow	as in cow	**atau**	*ah·tow*
ar	ahr	as in car	**bayar**	*bah·yar*
er	ər	er as in December	**berlibur, Desember**	*bər·lee·boor, deh·sehm·bər*
ir	eer	as in leer	**konfirmasi**	*kohn·feer·mah·see*
or	or	as in for	**paspor**	*pahs·por*

Consonants

Generally, consonants in the Indonesian language sound like their English counterparts:

b d f g h j k l m n p r s t v w y z.

The only exception is c, which sounds like 'ch' in 'charm'.

Letter	Symbol Used	Approximate Pronunciation	Example	Phonetic transcription
b	b	b as in but, web	**bawa, sebab**	*bah·wah, sah·bahb*
c	ch	ch as in church	**cuci**	*choo·chee*
d	d	d as in do, odd	**datang**	*dah·tahng*
f	f	f as in fool, leaf	**fasilitas**	*fah·see·lee·tahs*
g	g	g as in go, beg	**ganti**	*gahn·tee*
h	h	h as in ham, ahead	**hati, ramah**	*hah·tee, rah·mah*
j	j	j as in joy, judge	**jalan**	*jah·lahn*
k	k	k as in kiss, sick	**kamar**	*kah·mahr*
l	l	l as in leave, bell	**lain**	*lah·een*
m	m	m as in man, ham	**mau**	*mah·woo*
n	n	n as in no, tin	**nasi**	*nah·see*
p	p	p as in pin, tip	**pesan**	*pǝ·sahn*
r	r	r as in run, car	**ruang**	*roo·wahng*
s	s	s as in sun, miss	**saya, bisnis**	*sah·yah, biss·niss*
t	t	t as in too, bet	**tidak**	*tee·dahk*
w	w	w as in we	**waktu**	*wahk·too*
y	y	y as in yes	**ya**	*yah*
z	z	z as in zoo	**zaitun**	*zai·toon*
ng	ng	ng as in sing	**ruang**	*roo·wahng*

ny	ny	ny as in canyon	**nyanyi**	*nyah•nyee*
sy	**sh**	sh as in she, leash	**syal**	*syahl*

Note:

1. /g/ is always a hard /g/, as in 'go', never /j/ as in 'ginger'.
2. /h/ at the end of a syllable is always pronounced.
3. /c/ is always /ch/, as in 'church', never /k/ as in 'car' or /s/ as in 'certain'.

Consonant Combinations

Two consonant combinations are common in the Indonesian language.
The combination **ng** sounds like 'ng' in 'ring'. It can occur at the start, in the middle, or at the end of a word.

wide open (mouth) **nganga** *ngah•ngah*

hand **tangan** *tah•ngahn*

easy **senang** *sə•nahng*

*Take note that this combination is not equivalent to the sequence of 'n' followed by 'g' in the English word 'finger'. When this sequence of sounds is needed in Indonesian, it is spelt **nng** as in **tangguh**.

The combination **ny** sounds like 'ny' in 'banyan' or 'ni' in 'onion'. It can occur at the start or in the middle of a word.

fresh (environment) **nyaman** *nyah•mahn*

smile **senyum** *sə•nyoom*

In the Indonesian language, both '**anda**' and '**kamu**' refer to the pronoun 'you' and can be used interchangeably. However, '**anda**' is more polite whereas '**kamu**' is more casual. In a formal setting, '**anda**' is usually used. In this book, '**anda**' is used throughout for consistency.

How to use this Book

Sometimes you see two alternatives separated by a slash. Choose the one that's right for your situation.

ESSENTIAL

I'm on vacation
[holiday]/business.
Saya sedang berlibur/bisnis.
sah·yah sə·dahng ber·lee·boor/biss·niss

I'm going to...
Saya mau pergi ke...
sah·yah mah·woo pər·gee kə

I'm staying at the...
Hotel.
Saya tinggal di hotel...
sah·yah ting·gahl dee ho·tel

Words you may see are shown in YOU MAY SEE boxes.

YOU MAY SEE...

TUTUP *too·toop*   close
HAPUS *hah·poos*   delete

Any of the words or phrases listed can be plugged into the sentence below.

Online

Can I...?   **Boleh saya...?** *boh·leh sah·yah*
  access the internet   **mengakses internet** *mə·ngahk·ses in·tər·net*
  check e-mail   **cek e-mail** *check e-mail*
  print   **mencetak** *mən·cheh·tahk*

Indonesian phrases appear in purple.

Read the simplified pronunciation as if it were English. For more on pronunciation, see page 7.

Dining with Children

Do you have children's portions?

Ada porsi untuk anak kecil?
ahn·dah por·see oon·took ah·nahk kə·cheel

For Traveling with Children, see page 145.

Related phrases can be found by going to the page number indicated.

These are the emergency numbers in Indonesia.
Police : **110**
Fire department : **113**
Ambulance : **118**
Search and rescue team: **115**
These numbers can be accessed for free from all non-mobile telephones.
Major hotels offer medical services for minor ailments. A list of important numbers, including local emergency services, should be available at your hotel or local tourist information office.

Information boxes contain relevant country, culture and language tips.

Expressions you may hear are shown in You May Hear boxes.

YOU MAY HEAR...

Berikutnya! *bə·ree·koot·nyah*   Next!

Color-coded side bars identify each section of the book.

Survival

Arrival & Departure

ESSENTIAL

I'm on vacation [holiday]/business.	**Saya sedang berlibur/bisnis.** *sah·yah sə·dahng bər·lee·boor/biss·niss*
I'm going to...	**Saya mau pergi ke...** *sah·yah mah·woo pər·gee kə*
I'm staying at the... Hotel.	**Saya tinggal di hotel...** *sah·yah ting·gahl dee ho·tel*

YOU MAY HEAR...

Tolong, paspor anda. *toh·long, pahs·por ahn·dah.*	Your passport, please.
Apa tujuan/maksud kunjungan anda? *ah·pah too·joo·wahn/mahk·sood koon·joo·ngahn ahn·dah*	What's the purpose of your visit?
Anda tinggal di mana? *ahn·dah ting·gah dee mah·nah*	Where are you staying?
Anda akan tinggal berapa lama? *ahn·dah ah·kahn ting·gahl bə·rah·pah lah·mah*	How long are you staying?
Anda dengan siapa disini? *ahn·dah də·ngahn see·yah·pah dee·see·nee*	Who are you here with?

Border Control

I'm just passing through.	**Saya hanya singgah.** *sah·yah hah·nyah sing·gah*
I'd like to declare...	**Saya ingin melaporkan...** *sah·yah ee·ngin mə·lah·por·kahn*

| I have nothing to declare. | **Tidak ada yang harus dilaporkan.** *tee·dahk ah·dah y ahng hah·roos dee·lah·por·kahn* |

To enter Indonesia, you need a passport with at least six months between your date of entry to the expiry date of the passport. Citizens of Brunei, Chile, Hong Kong, Macao, Malaysia, Morocco, Peru, Philippines, Singapore, Thailand and Vietnam can enter the country without a visa (for a length of stay that is not longer than 30 days). Visitors from these countries can pay for and get a visa (for either three or 30 days) on arrival in Indonesia: Argentina, Australia, Austria, Belgium, Brazil, Canada, China, Denmark, Egypt, Finland, France, Germany, Hungary, India, Ireland, Italy, Japan, Kuwait, Luxembourg, Maldives, New Zealand, Norway, Poland, Portugal, Qatar, Russia, South Africa, South Korea, Saudi Arabia, Spain, Switzerland, the United Arab Emirates, the United Kingdom, and the United States of America. Visitors from other countries can apply for a single-entry social visa (valid for three months) at Indonesian diplomatic missions overseas.

YOU MAY HEAR...

Apakah ada yang ingin dilaporkan?
ah·pah·kah ah·dah yahng ee·ngin dee·lah·por·kahn

Anything to declare?

Anda harus membayar bea untuk ini.
ahn·dah hah·roos məm·bah·yar be·yah oon·took ee·nee

You must pay duty on this.

Buka tas ini. *boo·kah tahs ee·nee*

Open this bag.

YOU MAY SEE...

KEDATANGAN *kə·dah·tah·ngahn* arrival

KEBERANGKATAN *kə·bə·rahng·kah·tahn* departure

PABEAN/BEA-CUKAI *pah·be·yahn/ be·yah·coo·kye* customs

BARANG BEBAS PAJAK *bah·rahng beh·bahs pah·jahk* duty-free goods

BARANG YANG AKAN DILAPORKAN *bah·rahng yahng ah·kahn dee·lah·por·kahn* goods to declare

TIDAK ADA YANG DILAPORKAN *tee·dahk ah·dah yahng dee·lah·por·kahn* nothing to declare

KANTOR IMIGRASI immigration centre

POLISI *poh·lee·see* police

PEMERIKSAAN PASPOR *pə·məh·rik·sah·ahn pahs·por* passport control

Money

ESSENTIAL

Where's the…?	**…di mana?** *dee mah•nah*
ATM	**ATM** *ah•teh•em*
bank	**bank** *bahng*
foreign currency exchange counter	**tempat tukar uang asing/valas** *təm•paht too•kar oo•wahng ah•sing/vah•lahs*
When does the bank open/close?	**Kapan bank buka/tutup?** *kah•pahn bahng boo•kah/too•toop*
I'd like to change dollars/pounds into Rupiah.	**Saya ingin menukar dolar/pound ke Rupiah.** *sah•yah ee•ngin mə•noo•kar doh•lar/pound kə roo•pee•yah*
I'd like to cash traveler's checks [cheques].	**Saya ingin menguangkan cek wisata.** *sah•yah ee•ngin mə•ngoo•wahng•kahn check wee•sah•tah*

At the Bank

I'd like to change money/get a cash advance.	**Saya ingin menukar uang/ mendapatkan uang muka.** *sah•yah ee•ngin mə•noo•kar oo•wahng/ mən•dah•paht•kahn oo•wahng moo•kah*
What's the (foreign currency) exchange rate?	**Berapakah kurs tukar (valuta asing)?** *bə•rah•pah koors too•kar (vah•loo•tah ah•sing)*
I think there's a mistake.	**Saya rasa ada kesalahan.** *sah•yah rah•sah ah•dah kə•sah•lah•hahn*
I lost my traveler's checks [cheques].	**Saya kehilangan cek wisata.** *sah•yah kə•hee•lah•ngahn check wee•sah•tah*
The ATM ate my card.	**ATM menelan kartu saya.** *ah•teh•em mə•nə•lahn kar•too sah•yah*

My credit card…	**Kartu kredit saya…** kar·too kre·dit sah·yah
was lost	**hilang** hee·lahng
was stolen	**dicuri** dee·choo·ree
doesn't work	**tidak berfungsi** tee·dahk ber·foong·see

Carry a combination of cash and credit card and/or travelers' checks. Cash is imperative in rural areas, but you can change travelers' checks and use credit cards in established tourist areas. Travelers' checks are accepted at all banks. Major credit cards can be used at most hotels, department stores and some shops. A location that accepts credit card payment will display a credit card symbol in a visible place.

YOU MAY SEE…

MASUKKAN KARTU DI SINI   insert card here
mah·soo·kahn kar·too dee see·nee

BATAL bah·tahl   cancel

HAPUS hah·poos   clear

MASUKKAN mah·soo·kahn   insert

PIN pin   PIN

PENARIKAN pə·nah·ree·kahn   withdrawal

DARI REKENING KORAN/AKTIVA   from checking/
dah·ree reh·kə·ning koh·rahn/ahk·tee·vah   current account

DARI REKENING TABUNGAN   from savings account
dah·ree reh·kə·ning tah·boo·ngahn

RESI/TANDA TERIMA   receipt
rə·see/tahn·dah tə·ree·mah

The official name for Indonesia's monetary unit is **Indonesian Rupiah** (abbreviated **IDR**). The symbol used on all banknotes and coins is **Rp**. Coins come in six denominations: 25, 50, 100, 200, 500 and 1000 **Rupiah**. Banknotes are available in these denominations: **IDR**100, **IDR**500, **IDR**1,000, **IDR**5,000, **IDR**10,000, **IDR**20,000, **IDR**50,000, and **IDR**100,000.

Foreign currency can be converted at banks or licensed money changers, which operate beyond banking hours (most licensed money changers close at 8:00pm). Most currencies can be exchanged for **Rupiah**, but the popular ones are US dollars, pound sterling and Singapore dollars. Licensed money changers offer better rates than banks, while hotels and shopping centers levy an additional service charge (usually 10 to 20 percent). Exchange rates vary, so shop around.

ESSENTIAL

How do I get to town?	**Bagaimanakah cara menuju ke pusat kota?** *bah•gye•mah•nah•kah chah•rah mə•noo•joo kə poo•saht koh•tah*
Where's the…?	**…di mana?** *dee mah•nah*
airport	**bandara** *bahn•dah•rah*
train [railway] station	**stasiun kereta** *stah•see•yoon kə•reh•tah*
bus station	**stasiun bis** *stah•see•yoon bis*
How far is it?	**Seberapa jauh?** *sə•bə•rah•pah jah•wooh*
Where do I buy a ticket?	**Di mana saya membeli tiket?** *yah məm•bə•lee tee•ket*
A one-way/round-trip [return] ticket to…	**Tiket sekali jalan/pulang-pergi ke…** *tee•ket sə•kah•lee jah•lahn/poo•lahng•pər•gee kə*
How much?	**Berapa harganya?** *bə•rah•pah har•gah•nyah*
Which…?	**…yang mana?** *yahng mah•nah*
gate	**gerbang** *gər•bahng*
line	**jalur** *jah•loor*
platform	**peron** *peh•ron*
Where can I get a taxi?	**Di mana saya bisa mendapatkan taksi?** *dee mah•nah sah•yah bee•sah mən•dah•paht•kahn tahk•see*
Take me to this address.	**Antarkan saya ke alamat ini.** *ahn•tar•kahn sah•yah kə ah•lah•maht ee•nee*
Can I have a map?	**Boleh minta peta?** *boh•leh min•tah pə•tah*

Tickets

When's the...to Jakarta?	**Kapan...ke Jakarta?**	*kah·pahn... kə jah·kar·tah*
(first) bus	**bis (pertama)**	*bis (pər·tah·mah)*
(next) flight	**penerbangan (berikutnya)**	*pə·nər·bah·ngahn (bə·ree·koot·nyah)*
(last) train	**kereta (terakhir)**	*kə·reh·tah (tər·ah·kheer)*
Where do I buy a ticket?	**Di mana saya membeli tiket?**	*dee mah·nah sah·yah məm·bə·lee tee·ket*
One/two ticket(s), please.	**Tolong, tiketnya satu/dua.**	*toh·long, tee·ket·nyah sah·too/doo·wah*
For today/tomorrow.	**Untuk hari ini/besok.**	*oon·took hah·ree ee·nee/beh·sok*
A...ticket.	**Tiket...**	*tee·ket...*
one-way	**sekali jalan**	*sə·kah·lee jah·lahn*
return trip	**pulang pergi**	*poo·lahng pər·gee*
first class	**kelas satu**	*kə·lahs sah·too*
business class	**kelas bisnis**	*kə·lahs biss·niss*
economy class	**kelas ekonomi**	*kə·lahs eh·koh·noh·mee*
How much?	**Berapa harganya?**	*bə·rah·pah har·gah·nyah*
Is there a...discount?	**Apakah ada diskon untuk...?**	*ah·pah·kah ah·dah diss·kon oon·took*
child	**anak**	*ah·nahk*
student	**pelajar**	*pə·lah·jar*
senior citizen	**warga usia lanjut**	*war·gah oo·see·yah lahn·joot*
tourist	**turis**	*too·riss*
The express bus/express train, please.	**Bus ce·pat/kereta cepat.**	*bis chə·paht/kə·reh·tah chəh·paht*
The local bus/train, please.	**Kereta/bus lokal.**	*kə·reh·tah/bis loh·kahl*

YOU MAY HEAR...

Anda terbang dengan pesawat apa?
ahn·dah tər·bahng də·ngahn pə·sah·waht ah·pah

What airline are you flying?

Domestik atau internasional?
doh·mess·tick ah·tow in·tər·nah·shoh·nahl

Domestic or international?

Terminal mana? *tər·mee·nahl mah·nah*

What terminal?

I have an e-ticket.	**Saya punya e-ticket.** *sah·yah poo·nyah e-ticket*
Can I buy a ticket on the bus/train?	**Dapatkah saya membeli tiket di bis/kereta?** *dah·paht·kah sah·yah məm·bə·lee tee·ket dee bis/kə·reh·tah*
Do I have to stamp the ticket before boarding?	**Apakah saya harus mencap tiket sebelum naik kendaraan?** *ah·pah·kah sah·yah hah·roos mən·cahp tee·ket sə·bə·loom nah·yeek kən·dah·rah·ahn*
How long is this ticket valid?	**Berapa lama tiket ini berlaku?** *bə·rah·pah lah·mah tee·ket ee·nee bər·lah·koo*
Can I return on the same ticket?	**Dapatkah saya kembali dengan tiket yang sama?** *dah·paht·kah sah·yah kəm·bah·lee də·ngahn tee·ket yahng sah·mah*
I'd like…my reservation.	**Saya ingin…reservasi saya.** *sah·yah ee·ngin… re·ser·vah·see sah·yah*
to cancel	**membatalkan** *məm·bah·tahl·kahn*
to change	**mengubah** *mə·ngoo·bah*
to confirm	**mengkonfirmasi** *mang·kohn·feer·mah·see*

For Days, see page 171.

For Time, see page 171.

Indonesia is well-connected by several airlines to all continents. Most visitors arrive by air at one of the 17 international airports located on the main islands of the country. The capital city Jakarta (on the island of Java) is served by the Soekarno-Hatta International Airport. Most domestic airports are serviced by Garuda Indonesia (the national carrier) and AirAsia (a budget airline). Tickets can be booked in advance through the individual company websites or through your local travel agent. (Airport tax and surcharges apply).

Plane

Airport Transfer

How much is a taxi to the airport?	**Berapa biaya taksi ke bandara?** *bə·rah·pah bee·yah·yah tahk·see kə bahn·dah·rah*
To…Airport, please.	**Tolong antarkan ke Bandara…** *toh·long ahn·tar·kahn kə bahn·dah·rah*
My airline is…	**Pesawat saya…** *pə·sah·waht sah·yah*
My flight leaves at…	**Pesawat saya berangkat jam…** *pə·sah·waht sah·yah bə·rahng·kaht jahm*
I'm in a rush.	**Saya terburu-buru.** *sah·yah tər·boo·roo·boo·roo*
Can you take an alternate route?	**Bisa ambil rute alternatif/rute lain?** *bee·sah ahm·beel roo·tə ahl·tər·nah·teef/roo·tə lah·yeen*
Can you drive faster/slower?	**Bisa jalan lebih cepat/perlahan?** *bee·sah jah·lahn lə·beeh cə·paht/pər·lah·hahn*

Checking In

Where's check-in?	**Check-in di mana?** *check-in dee mah·nah*
My name is…	**Nama saya…** *nah·mah sah·yah*
I'm going to…	**Saya mau pergi ke…** *sah·yah mah·woo pər·gee kə*
I have…	**Saya punya…** *sah·yah poo·nyah*

YOU MAY SEE...

KEDATANGAN *kə•dah•tah•ngahn*	arrivals
KEBERANGKATAN *kə•bə•rahng•kah•tahn*	departures
AMBIL KOPER/BAGASI *ahm•beel koh•pər/bah•gah•see*	baggage claim
KEAMANAN/SEKURITI/ SATPAM *kə•ah•mah•nahn/sə•koo•ree•tee/saht•pahm*	security
PENERBANGAN DOMESTIK *pə•nər•bah•ngahn doh•mess•tick*	domestic flights
PENERBANGAN INTERNASIONAL *pə•nər•bah•ngahn in•tər•nah•shoh•nahl*	international flights
CHECK-IN *check-in*	check-in
CHECK-IN E-TICKET *check-in e-ticket*	e-ticket check-in
PINTU KEBERANGKATAN *pin•too kə•bə•rahng•kah•tahn*	departure gates
BANDARA *bahn•dah•rah*	airport
PESAWAT TERBANG *pə•sah•waht tər•bahng*	airplane

one suitcase	**satu koper** *sah•too koh•por*
two suitcases	**dua koper** *doo•wah koh•por*
one piece of hand luggage	**satu tas jinjing** *sah•too tahs jin•jing*
How much luggage is allowed?	**Berapa banyak koper yang diperbolehkan?** *bə•rah•pah bah•nyahk koh•por yahng dee•pər•boh•leh•kahn*
Is that pounds or kilos?	**Itu dalam pon atau kilo?** *ee•too dah•lahm pound ah•tow kee•loh*

Which terminal/ gate?	**Terminal/Pintu mana?** *tər·mee·nahl/pin·too mah·nah*
I'd like a window/an aisle seat.	**Saya ingin tempat duduk dekat jendela/di pinggir.** *sah·yah ee·ngin təm·paht doo·dook də·kaht jan·de·lah/dee ping·geer*
When do we leave/ arrive?	**Kapan kami berangkat/tiba?** *kah·pahn kah·mee bə·rahng·kaht/tee·bah*
Is the flight delayed?	**Apakah penerbangannya ditunda?** *ah·pah·kah pə·nər·bah·ngahn·nyah dee·toon·dah*
How late?	**Sampai kapan?** *sahm·pye kah·pahn*

Luggage

Where is/are…?	**…di mana?** *dee mah·nah*
the luggage trolleys	**kereta koper [troli]** *kə·reh·tah koh·por [tro·lee]*
the luggage lockers	**loker untuk koper** *loh·kher oon·took koh·por*
the baggage claim	**tempat mengambil koper** *təm·paht mə·ngahm·beel koh·por*
My luggage has been lost/stolen.	**Koper saya hilang/dicuri.** *koh·por sah·yah hee·ahng/dee·choo·ree*

YOU MAY HEAR...

Berikutnya! *bə•ree•koot•nyah*

Next!

Paspor/Tiket anda. *pahs•por/ tee•ket ahn•dah*

Your passport/ticket, please.

Apakah anda ada koper yang ingin dimasukkan bagasi? *ah•pah•kah ahn•dah ah•dah koh•por yahng ee•ngin dee•mah•soo•kahn bah•gah•see*

Are you checking any luggage?

Itu terlalu besar untuk dijinjing [untuk dibawa ke pesawat]. *ee•too ltər•lah•oo bə•sar oon•took dee•jin•jing [oon•took dee•bah•wah kə pə•sah•waht]*

That's too large for a carry-on [to carry on board].

Apakah anda sendiri yang membereskan koper? *ah•pah•kah ahn•dah sən•dee•ree yahng məm•beh•ress•kahn koh•por*

Did you pack these bags yourself?

Apakah ada yang menitipkan sesuatu kepada anda untuk dibawa? *ah•pah•kah ah•dah yahng mə•nee•tip•kahn sə•soo•wah•too kə•pah•dah ahn•dah oon•took dee•bah•wah*

Did anyone give you anything to carry?

Keluarkan isi saku anda. *kə•loo•wahr•kahn ee•see sah•koo ahn•dah*

Empty your pockets.

Buka sepatu anda. *boo•kah sə•pah•too ahn•dah*

Take off your shoes.

Silahkan naik ke pesawat... *see•lah•kahn nah•yeek kə pə•sah•what*

Now boarding...

My suitcase is damaged.

Koper/tas saya rusak. *koh•por/tahs sah•yah roo•sahk*

Finding your Way

Where is/are...?	**...di mana?** *dee mah·nah*
the foreign	**menukar mata uang asing**
currency exchange	*mə·noo·kar mah·tah oo·wahng ah·sing*
the car hire	**menyewa mobil** *mə·nyeh·wah moh·beel*
the exit	**pintu keluar** *pin·too kə·loo·wahr*
the taxis	**taksi** *tahk·see*
Is there a...into	**Apakah ada...yang ke pusat kota?**
town?	*ah·pah·kah ah·dah...yahng kə poo·saht koh·tah*
bus	**bis** *bis*
train	**kereta api** *kə·reh·tah ah·pee*

Train

Where's the train	**Stasiun kereta di mana?**
station?	*stah·see·yoon kə·reh·tah dee mah·nah*
How far is it?	**Seberapa jauh?** *sə·bə·rah·pah jah·wooh*
Where is/are...?	**Di mana...?** *dee mah·nah*
the ticket office	**loket tiket** *loh·ket tee·ket*
the information	**tempat informasi** *təm·paht in·for·mah·see*
desk	

YOU MAY SEE...

PERON *peh·ron*	platforms
INFORMASI *in·for·mah·see*	information
RESERVASI *reh·ser·vah·see*	reservations
RUANG TUNGGU *roo·wahng toong·goo*	waiting room
KEDATANGAN *kə·dah·tah·ngahn*	arrivals
KEBERANGKATAN *kə·bə·rahng·kah·tahn*	departures

the luggage lockers	**loker koper** *loh·kher koh·por*
the platforms	**peron** *peh·ron*
Can I have a schedule [timetable]?	**Boleh minta jadwal?** *boh·leh min·tah jahd·wahl*
Is it a direct train?	**Apakah ini kereta api langsung?** *ah·pah·kah ee·nee kə·reh·tah ah·pee lahng·soong*
Do I have to change trains?	**Apakah saya harus ganti kereta?** *ah·pah·kah sah·yah hah·roos gahn·tee kə·reh·tah*

Traveling by train is inexpensive in Indonesia. **PT Kereta Api** (**Persero**) offers rail services throughout the country (although most of their lines are located on the island of Java). **KRL Jabotabek** operates commuter lines in the Jakarta area. Train services are divided into three classes. The Executive class is spacious and air-conditioned but it's only available on principal expresses. The Business and Economy classes are not air-conditioned. Both Executive and Business classes are equipped with reclining seats, while the Economy class is fitted with benches. Tickets can be booked online, up to 30 days in advance.

YOU MAY HEAR...

Penumpang silakan naik!   All aboard!
pə·noom·pahng see·lah·kahn nah·yeek

Tolong, tiketnya. *tho·long tee·ket·nyah*   Tickets, please.

Anda harus ganti kereta di Jakarta.   You have to change at
ahn·dah hah·roos gahn·tee kə·reh·tah   Jakarta.
dee jah·kar·tah

Pemberhentian berikutnya, Bandung.   Next stop, Bandung.
pəm·bər·hən·tee·yahn bə·ree·koot·nyah,
bahn·doong

How long is the trip?	**Berapa lama perjalanannya?** *bə·rah·pah lah·mah* *pər·jah·lah·nahn·nyah*
Is the train on time?	**Apakah keretanya tepat waktu?** *ah·pah·kah kə·* *reh·tah·nyah tə·paht wahk·too*

For Asking Directions, see page 37.

For Tickets, see page 20.

Departures

Which track [platform] to...?	**Jalur [peron] mana untuk ke...?** *jah·loor [peh·ron] mah·nah oon·took kə*
Is this the track [platform]/train to...?	**Apakah ini jalur [peron]/kereta menuju ke...?** *ah·pah·kah ee·nee jah·loor [peh·ron]/kə·reh·tah* *mə·noo·joo kə*
Where is track [platform]...?	**Jalur [peron]...di mana?** *jah·loor [peh·ron]...* *dee mah·nah*
Where do I change for...?	**Di mana saya ganti/tukar...?** *dee mah·nah* *sah·yah gahn·tee/too·khar*

On Board

Can I sit here?	**Boleh saya duduk disini?**	boh·leh sah·yah doo·dook dee see·nee
Can I open the window?	**Boleh saya buka jendela?**	boh·leh sah·yah boo·kah jən·de·lah
That's my seat.	**Itu tempat duduk saya**.	ee·too təm·paht doo·dook sah·yah
Here's my reservation.	**Ini reservasi saya.**	ee·nee reh·ser·vah·see sah·yah

Bus

Where's the bus station?	**Stasiun bis di mana?**	stah·see·yoon bis dee mah·nah
How far is it?	**Seberapa jauh?**	sə·bə·rah·pah jah·wooh
How do I get to…?	**Bagaimana saya menuju ke…?**	bah·gye·mah·nah sah·yah mə·noo·joo kə
Is this the bus to…?	**Apakah bis ini menuju ke…?**	ah·pah·kah bis ee·nee mə·noo·joo kə
Can you tell me when to get off?	**Bisa beri tahu saya kapan harus turun dari bis?**	bee·sah bə·ree tah·woo sah·yah kah·pahn hah·roos too·roon dah·ree bis

---

YOU MAY SEE…

PEMBERHENTIAN BIS	bus stop
pəm·bər·hən·tee·yahn bis	
BERHENTI bər·hən·tee	request stop
MASUK/KELUAR mah·sook/ kə·loo·wahr	enter/exit
TUNJUKKAN TIKET ANDA toon·jook·kahn tee·keht ahn·dah	stamp your ticket

There are generally four types of bus services in Indonesia public buses that operate within a city; inter-city and inter-province buses; tour buses for sightseeing; and '**Busway**' (air-conditioned public buses that are quite comfortable, but which only operate in Jakarta).

Bus fares in Indonesia are inexpensive, and non air-conditioned buses are usually packed (despite the warm weather) as they charge less than the air-conditioned ones. However, bus drivers can be somewhat reckless.

Do I have to change buses?	**Apakah saya harus ganti bis?** *ah•pah•kah sah•yah hah•roos gahn•tee bis*
How many stops to…?	**Berapa kali berhenti sampai ke…?** *bə•rah•pah kah•lee bər•hən•tee sahm•pye kə*
Stop here, please!	**Stop di sini!** *stop dee see•nee*

For Tickets, see page 20.

Boat & Ferry

When is the ferry to…?	**Kapan feri ke…?** *kah•pahn feh•ree kə*
Can I take my car?	**Bisakah saya membawa mobil?** *bee•sah•kah sah•yah məm•bah•wah mo•beel*
Where are the life jackets?	**Jaket pelampung di mana?** *jah•ket pə•lahm•poong dee mah•nah*
What time is the next sailing?	**Pukul berapa pelayaran berikutnya?** *poo•kool bə•rah•pah pə•lah•yahr•ahn bə•ree•koot•nyah*
Can I book a seat/cabin?	**Bisakah saya memesan tempat/kabin?** *bee•sah•kah sah•yah mə•mə•sahn tam•paht/kah•been*
How long is the crossing?	**Berapa lama waktu penyeberangan?** *bə•rah•pah lah•mah wahk•too pə•nyə•bə•rahng•ahn*

Traveling in and around Indonesia's capital city Jakarta has been made easier with the availability of commuter train services operated by **KRL Jabotabek**. Several rail lines connect Jakarta to neighboring regions as well.

Most islands in Indonesia can be visited by boat and ferry from the major coastal towns. However, in the monsoon season (November to March) ferry services may sometimes be disrupted by bad weather. Note that the sea can be choppy just before and after the monsoon period.

YOU MAY SEE...

PERAHU SEKOCI *pə•rah•hoo sə•koh•chee*		life boat
JAKET PELAMPUNG *jah•ket pə•lahm•poong*		life jacket

Taxi

Where can I get a taxi?	**Di mana saya bisa mendapatkan taksi?** *dee mah•nah sah•yah bee•sah mən•dah•paht•kahn tahk•see*
Can you send a taxi?	**Bisakah Anda mengirimkan taksi?** *bee•sah•kah ahn•dah mə•ngee•reem•kahn tahk•see*
Do you have the number for a taxi?	**Anda punya nomor telepon untuk pesan taksi?** *ahn•dah poo•nyah noh•mor tə•lə•pohn oon•took pə•sahn tahk•see*
I'd like a taxi now/for tomorrow at (time)...	**Saya perlu taksi sekarang/besok jam...** *sah•yah pər•loo tahk•see sə•kah•rahng/beh•sok jahm*

Taxis, mostly air-conditioned, are readily available and fares are metered if the cabbie decides not to use the meter. Negotiate the fare before boarding. In cities, taxis can be found at taxi stands or flagged down anywhere. Taxis can be hired by the hour or contracted to travel long-distance across towns or regions of the larger islands. There are several companies offering taxi services in Indonesia — **Silver Bird** and **Blue Bird** come recommended. Tipping is not common in Indonesia, but tips offered will be happily accepted.

Cars, limousines and minibuses can also be rented for a reasonable fee.

YOU MAY HEAR...

Kemana? *kə•mah•nah*
Where to?

Alamatnya di mana? *ah•lah•maht•nyah dee mah•nah*
What's the address?

Ada biaya tambahan untuk malam hari/ke bandara. *ah•dah bee•yah•yah tahm•bah•hahn oon•took mah•lahm hah•ree/ kə bahn•dah•rah*
There's a night time/ airport surcharge.

I'm going to...	**Saya mau pergi ke...** *sah•yah mah•woo pər•gee kə*
this address	**alamat ini** *ah•lah•maht ee•nee*
the airport	**bandara** *bahn•dah•rah*
the train station	**stasiun kereta api** *stah•see•yoon kə•reh•tah ah•pee*
I'm late.	**Saya terlambat.** *sah•yah tər•lahm•baht*

Can you drive faster/slower?	**Bisa jalan lebih cepat/perlahan?** *bee•sah jah•lahn lə•beeh cə•paht/par•lah•hahn*
Stop/Wait here.	**Stop/Tunggu disini.** *stop/toong•goo dee•see•nee*
How much?	**Berapa ongkosnya?** *bə•rah•pah ong•kos•nyah*
You said it would cost…	**Anda bilang ongkosnya…** *ahn•dah bee•lahng ong•kos•nyah*
Keep the change.	**Ambil kembaliannya.** *ahm•beel kəm•bah•lee•yahn•nyah*

Bicycle, Motorbike & Trishaw

I'd like to hire…	**Saya ingin menyewa [sewa]…** *sah•yah ee•ngin mə•nyeh•wah*
a bicycle	**sepeda** *sə•peh•dah*
a motorcycle	**sepeda motor** *sə•peh•dah moh•tor*
a trishaw	**becak/bajaj** *beh•chahk/bah•jye*
How much per day/week?	**Berapa biaya per hari/minggu?** *bə•rah•pah bee•yah•yah par hah•ree/ming•goo*
Can I have a helmet/lock?	**Boleh minta helm/kunci?** *boh•leh min•tah heh•ləm/koon•chee*

Bicycle and motorcycle rentals are not popular in Indonesia. They are usually only available at parks or recreational areas. Trishaws and autorickshaws (**bajaj**) are available for hire in many cities, but are banned from most parts of Jakarta. You will need to agree to a price with the driver before you get on. Rides within the city or town vary according to the distance.

YOU MAY HEAR...

Anda punya SIM (surat izin mengemudi) internasional? *ahn·dah poo·nyah sim (soo·raht ee·zin mə·ngə·moo·dee) in·tər·nah·shoh·nahl*	Do you have an international driver's license?
Tolong, paspornya. *oh·long pahs·por·nyaht*	Your passport, please.
Anda ingin asuransi? *ahn·dah ee·ngin ah·soo·rahn·see*	Do you want insurance?
Saya perlu uang muka. *sah·yah pər·loo oo·wahng moo·kah*	I'll need a deposit.
Paraf/Tanda tangan di sini. *pah·rahf/ Tahn·dahtah·ngahn dee see·nee*	Initial/Sign here.

Car Hire

Where's the car hire?	**Tempat menyewa mobil di mana?** *tem·paat mə·nyeh·wah moh·beel dee mah·nah*
I'd like...	**Saya mau...** *sah·yah mah·woo*
a cheap/small car	**mobil yang murah/kecil** *moh·beel yahng moo·rah/ kə·cheel*

Car rentals are available for those keen on self-drive trips. Several car hire companies, including some international names such as Avis and Hertz, are based in major cities and listed in the Yellow Pages. You will also find car hire counters at major airports. To drive in Indonesia, you must be over 17 years of age, and you need an international driving licence. Indonesia uses right-hand drive cars, which means that traffic keeps to the left-hand side of the road. Take note that about half the roads in Indonesia are unpaved, so the ride could get bumpy. In some places, you may even run into the occasional ox-drawn cart.

an automatic/ a manual car	**mobil otomatis/manual** *moh·beel oh·toh·mah·tees/mah·noo·wah*
air conditioning	**ber-AC** *bər·ah·seh*
a child's car seat	**tempat duduk anak di mobil** *təm·paht doo·dook* *ah·nahk dee moh·beel*
How much…?	**Berapa…?** *bə·rah·pah*
per day/week	**per hari/minggu** *pər hah·ree/ming·goo*
per kilometer	**per kilometer** *pər kee·loh·meh·tər*
for unlimited mileage	**untuk jarak tanpa batas** *oon·took jah·rahk tahn·pah* *ba·tahs*
with insurance	**dengan asuransi** *də·ngahn ah·soo·rahn·see*
Are there any discounts?	**Ada diskon?** *ah·dah diss·kohn*

YOU MAY SEE...

BENSIN *ben·sin*	gas [petrol]
BERTIMBAL *bər·tim·bahl*	leaded
BEBAS TIMBAL *beh·bahs tim·bahl*	unleaded
BIASA *bee·yah·sah*	regular
SOLAR *soh·lahr*	diesel
SWALAYAN *swah·lah·yahn*	self-service
LAYANAN LENGKAP *lah·yah·nahn ləng·kahp*	full-service

Fuel Station

Where's the fuel station?	**Pompa bensin di mana?** *pohm·pah ben·sind dee mah·nah*
Fill it up.	**Isi penuh.** *ee·see pə·nooh*
… euros, please.	**… dalam euro saja.** *dah·lahm yoo·roh sah·jah*
I'll pay in cash/by credit card.	**Saya bayar kontan/pakai kartu kredit.** *sah·yah bah·yahr kon·tahn/pah·kye kar·too kre·dit*

YOU MAY HEAR...

lurus *loo·roos*	straight ahead
belok *beh·lohk*	turn
kiri *kee·ree*	left
kanan *kah·nahn*	right
pada/di balik tikungan	on/around the corner
pah-dah/dee bah·leek tee·koo·ngahn	
di seberang *dee sə·bə·rahng*	opposite
di belakang *dee bə·lah·kahng*	behind
di samping *dee sahm·ping*	next to
setelah *sə·tə·lah*	after
utara/selatan *oo·tah·rah/sə·lah·tahn*	north/south
timur/barat *tee·moor/bah·raht*	east/west
pada lampu lalu lintas *pah·dah*	at the traffic light
lahm·poo lah·loo lin·tahs	
di persimpangan *dee pər·sim·pah·ngahn*	at the intersection

Asking Directions

Is this the way to...?	**Apakah ini jalan menuju ke...?**
	ah·pah·kah ee·nee jah·lahn mə·noo·joo kə
How far is it to...?	**Seberapa jauh ke...?** *sə·bə·rah·pah jah·wooh kə*
Where's...?	**Di mana...?** *dee mah·nah*
...Street	**Jalan...** *ah·lahn*
this address	**alamat ini** *ah·lah·maht ee·nee*
the highway	**jalan besar** *jah·lahn bə·sar*
Can you show me	**Bisa anda tunjukkan pada peta?** *bee·sah ahn·dah*
on the map?	*toon·joo·kahn pah·dah pə·tah*
I'm lost.	**Saya kesasar.** *sah·yah kə·sah·sar*

YOU MAY SEE...

ALAN MASUK *jah·lahn mah·sook*	entrance
KELUAR *kə·loo·wahr*	exit
PERLAHAN *pər·lah·hahn*	slow
BERI JALAN *bə·ree jah·lahn*	yield

Parking

Can I park here?	**Boleh saya parkir di sini?** *boh·leh sah·yah par·keer dee see·nee*
Where's the...?	**...di mana?** *dee mah·nah*
parking lot [car park]	**pelataran parkir** *pə·lah·tah·rahn par·keer*
parking garage	**tempat parkir** *təm·paht pahr·kir*
parking meter	**meteran parkir** *meh·tə·rahn par·keer*
How much...?	**Berapa...?** *bə·rah·pah*
per hour	**per jam** *pər jahm*
per day	**per hari** *pər hah·ree*
overnight	**semalaman** *sə·mah·lah·mahn*

Breakdown & Repair

My car broke down/ won't start.	**Mobil saya mogok/tidak bisa start.** *moh·beel sah·yah moh·gok/tee·dahk bee·sah start*
Can you fix it?	**Anda bisa perbaiki?** *ahn·dah bee·sah pər·bah·yee·kee*

Ikatan Motor Indonesia (IMI) is the national motoring organisation in Indonesia. It has offices in most major cities, and provides a prompt breakdown service for members. The official website is www.imi.co.id

When will it be ready?	**Kapan selesai?** *kah•pahn sə•lə•sye*
How much?	**Berapa ongkosnya?** *bə•rah•pah ong•kos•nyah*
I have a puncture	**Ban saya bocor/kempis.** *bahn sah•yah boh•chohr/ kəm•pees.*

Accidents

| There was an accident. | **Ada kecelakaan.** *ah•dah kə•chə•lah•kah•ahn* |
| Call an ambulance/ the police. | **Panggil ambulan/polisi.** *pahng•geel ahm•boo•lahn/ poh•lee•see* |

Places to Stay

ESSENTIAL

Can you recommend a hotel?	**Hotel apa yang anda sarankan?** *hoh•tell ah•pah yahng ahn•dah sah•rahn•kahn*
I have a reservation.	**Saya punya reservasi.** *sah•yah poo•nyah re•ser•vah•see*
My name is...	**Nama saya...** *nah•mah sah•yah*

Do you have a room…?	**Ada kamar…?** *Ah·dah kah·mar*
for one/two	**untuk satu/dua orang** *oon·took sah·too/doo·wah oh·rahng*
with a bathroom	**dengan kamar mandi** *də·ngahn kah·mar mahn·dee*
with air conditioning	**dengan AC** *də·ngahn ah·seh*
For…	**Untuk…** *oon·took*
tonight	**malam ini** *mah·lahm ee·nee*
two nights	**dua malam** *doo·wah mah·lahm*
one week	**satu minggu** *sah·too ming·goo*
How much?	**Berapa?** *bə·rah·pah*
Is there anything cheaper?	**Ada yang lebih murah?** *ah·dah yahng lə·beeh moo·rah*
When's check-out?	**Kapan waktu check-out?** *kah·pahn wahk·too check-out*
Can I leave this in the safe?	**Bisa saya simpan ini dalam lemari besi?** *bee·sah sah·yah sim·pahn ee·nee dah·lahm lə·mah·ree bə·see*
Can I leave my bags (here)?	**Boleh saya tinggalkan tas saya (disini)?** *boh·leh sah·yah ting·gahl·kahn tahs sah·yah (dee·see·nee)*
Can I have my bill/a receipt?	**Boleh minta bon/kwitansi?** *boh·leh min·tah bon/kwee·tahn·see*
I'll pay in cash/by credit card.	**Saya bayar kontan/pakai kartu kredit.** *sah·yah bah·yahr kon·tahn/pah·kye kar·too kre·dit*

Somewhere to Stay

Can you recommend…?	**Dapatkah anda menyarankan…?** *dah•paht•kah ahn•dah mə•nyah•rahn•kahn*
a hotel	**hotel** *hoh•tell*
a hostel	**losmen** *los•men*
a campsite	**tempat berkemah** *təm•paht bər•keh•mah*
What is it near?	**Dekat mana?** *də•kaht mah•nah*
How do I get there?	**Bagaimana saya ke sana?** *bah•gye•mah•nah sah•yah kə sah•nah*

At the Hotel

| I have a reservation. | **Saya punya reservasi.** *sah•yah poo•nyah reh•ser• vah•see* |
| My name is… | **Nama saya…** *nah•mah sah•yah* |

In Indonesia, accommodation options range from five-star luxury hotels run by international chains to the modest but adequate **rumah kost** (lodging house), usually a residential home that rents out rooms on a monthly basis. The government regulates the industry by issuing licences to operate hotels and to sell alcohol. Most properties are rated by stars (1-5).

International-standard hotels are found in the major cities and popular holiday spots, with good service, marble floors, thick-pile carpets, discos, live entertainment, swimming pools and restaurants serving Western, Chinese, Japanese or local food. Rack rates can be as high as IDR 3,000,000 and above, but most average around IDR 350,000 upwards. Two- or three-star hotels are basic, many with air-conditioning, and most are safe.

YOU MAY HEAR...

Tolong, paspor/ kartu kredit anda.
toh•long pahs•por/kar•too kre•dit ahn•dah
Isi formulir ini. *ee•see for•moo•leer ee•nee*
Tanda tangan disini. *tahn•dah tah•ngahn dee•see•nee*

Your passport/credit card, please.
Fill out this form.
Sign here.

Do you have a room...?	**Anda punya kamar...?** *ahn•dah poo•nyah kah•mar*
with a bathroom [toilet]/shower	**dengan kamar mandi [WC]/shower** *də•ngahn kah•mar mahn•dee [weh•reh]/shower*
with air conditioning	**dengan AC** *də•ngahn ah•seh*
that's smoking/ non-smoking	**yang boleh merokok/tidak merokok** *yahng boh•leh mə•roh•kohk/tee•dahk mə•roh•kohk*
For...	**Untuk...** *oon•took*
tonight	**malam ini** *mah•lahm ee•nee*
two nights	**dua malam** *doo•wah mah•lahm*
a week	**satu minggu** *sah•too ming•goo*
Do you have...?	**Anda punya...?** *ahn•dah poo•nyah*
a computer	**komputer** *kohm•poo•tər*
an elevator [a lift]	**lift** *lift*
(wireless) internet service	**layanan internet (nirkabel)** *lah•yah•nahn in•tər•net (nir•kah•bəl)*
room service	**room service** *room service*
a TV	**TV** *tee•fee*
a pool	**kolam renang** *koh•lahm rə•nahng*
a gym	**ruang olahraga** *roo•wahng oh•lah•rah•gah*

I need…	**Saya perlu…** *sah•yah pər•loo*
an extra bed	**tempat tidur ekstra** *təm•paht tee•door eks•trah*
a cot/crib	**buaian/tempat tidur bayi** *boo•wye•yahn/təm•paht tee•door bah•yee*

For Numbers, see page 169.

Price

How much per night/week?	**Berapa biaya per malam/minggu?** *bə•rah•pah bee•yah•yah pər mah•lahm/ming•goo*
Does that include breakfast/sales tax?	**Apakah itu termasuk sarapan/ pajak penjualan?** *ah•pah•kah ee•too tər•mah•sook sah•rah•pahn/ pah•jahk pən•joo•wah•lahn*
Are there any discounts?	**Ada diskon?** *ah•dah diss•kon*

Preferences

Can I see the room?	**Boleh saya lihat kamarnya?** *boh•leh sah•yah lee•haht kah•mar•nyah*
I'd like a…room.	**Saya ingin kamar yang…** *sah•yah ee•ngin kah•mar yahng*
better	**lebih baik** *lə•beeh bah•yeek*

bigger	**lebih besar** *lə·beeh bə·sar*	
cheaper	**lebih murah** *lə·beeh moo·rah*	
quieter	**lebih tenang** *lə·beeh tə·nahng*	
I'll take it.	**Saya ambil yang ini.** *sah·yah ahm·beel yahng ee·nee*	
No, I won't take it.	**Tidak, saya tidak mau kamar ini.** *tee·dahk, sah·yah tee·dahk mah·woo kah·mar ee·nee*	

Questions

Where's the…?	**…di mana?** *dee mah·nah*	
bar	**bar** *bar*	
bathroom [toilet]	**kamar mandi** *kah·mar mahn·dee*	
elevator [lift]	**lift** *lift*	
Can I have…?	**Boleh saya minta…?** *boh·leh sah·yah min·tah*	
a blanket	**selimut** *sə·lee·moot*	
an iron	**setrika** *sə·tree·kah*	
the room key/ key card	**kunci/kartu kunci kamar** *koon·chee/kar·too koon·chee kah·mar*	
a pillow	**bantal** *bahn·tahl*	
soap	**sabun** *sah·boon*	
toilet paper	**kertas WC** *kər·tahs weh·seh*	
a towel	**handuk** *hahn·dook*	

The voltage used in Indonesia is 220, alternating at 50 Hertz or cycles per second. Outlets in Indonesia generally accept two types of plugs — two round pins, or two parallel flat pins and a ground pin. You may need a voltage or plug adapter for any appliances and electronics brought into Indonesia.

YOU MAY SEE...

DORONG/TARIK _doh•rong/tah•reek_	push/pull
KAMAR MANDI _kah•mar mahn•dee_	bathroom [toilet]
TANGGA _tahng•gah_	stairs
MESIN ES _mə•sin es_	ice machines
MESIN VENDING _mə•sin ven•ding_	vending machines
LAUNDRY [CUCI BAJU] _lawn•dree choo•cee ba•joo_	laundry
JANGAN GANGGU _jah•ngahn gahng•goo_	do not disturb
PINTU KELUAR KEBAKARAN _pin•too kə•loo• wahr ke•bha•kar•an_	fire door
PINTU KELUAR (DARURAT) _pin•too kə•loo•wahr (dah•roo•raht)_	(emergency) exit
PANGGILAN UNTUK BANGUN _pahng•gee•lahn oon•took bah•ngoon_	wake-up call

Do you have an adapter for this?	**Anda punya adaptor untuk ini?** _ahn•dah poo•nyah ah•dahp•tor oon•took ee•nee_
How do I turn on the lights?	**Bagaimana cara menyalakan lampu?** _bah•gye•mah•nah chah•rah mə•nyah•lah•kahn lahm•poo_
Can you wake me at…?	**Bisa bangunkan saya jam...?** _bee•sah bah•ngoon•kahn sah•yah jahm_
Can I leave this in the safe?	**Bisa saya simpan ini dalam lemari besi?** _bee•sah sah•yah sim•pahn ee•nee dah•lahm lə•mah•ree bə•see_

Can I have my things from the safe?	**Bisa tolong ambilkan barang saya dari lemari besi?** *bee·sah toh·lohng ahm·beel·kahn bah·rahng sah·yah dah·ree lə·mah·ree bə·see*
Is there mail [post]/message for me?	**Apakah ada surat/pesan untuk saya?** *ah·pah·kah ah·dah soo·raht/pə·sahn oon·took sah·yah*
What time do you lock up?	**Jam berapa anda tutup?** *jahm bə·rah·pah ahn·dah too·toop*
Do you have a laundry service?	**Anda punya layanan penatu?** *ahn·dah poo·nyah lah·yahn·ahn pə·nah·too*

Problems

There's a problem.	**Ada masalah.** *ah·dah mah·sah·lah*
I lost my key/key card.	**Saya kehilangan kunci/kartu kunci.** *sah·yah kə·hee·lah·ngahn koon·chee/kar·too koon·chee*
I'm locked out of the room.	**Saya tidak bisa masuk ke kamar.** *sah·yah tee·dahk bee·sah mah·sook kə kah·mar*
There's no hot water/toilet paper.	**Tidak ada air panas/kertas WC.** *tee·dahk ah·dah ah·yeer pah·nahs/kər·tahs weh·seh*
The room is dirty.	**Kamarnya kotor.** *kah·mar·nyah koh·tor*
There are bugs in the room.	**Ada kecoa di kamar.** *ah·dah kə·choh·wah dee kah·mar*
The...doesn't work.	**...tidak berfungsi.** *tee·dahk ber·foong·see*
Can you fix the...?	**Anda bisa perbaiki...?** *ahn·dah bee·sah pər·bah·yee·kee*
air conditioning	**AC** *ah·seh*
fan	**kipas angin** *kee·pahs ah·ngin*
heater	**alat pemanas** *ah·laht pə·mah·nahs*
light	**lampu** *lahm·poo*
TV	**TV** *tee·fee*
toilet	**WC** *weh·seh*
I'd like another room.	**Saya ingin kamar yang lain.** *sah·yah ee·ngin kah·mar yahng lah·yeen*

Checking Out

When's check-out (time)?	**Kapan waktu check-out?** *kah•pahn wahk•too check-out*
Can I leave my bags here until…?	**Boleh saya tinggalkan tas saya di sini sampai…?** *boh•leh sah•yah ting•gahl•kahn tahs sah•yah dee see•nee sahm•pye*
Can I have an itemized bill/a receipt?	**Boleh minta perincian bon/kwitansi?** *boh•leh min•tah pə•rin•chee•yahn bon/kwee•tahn•see*
I think there's a mistake.	**Saya rasa ada kesalahan.** *sah•yah rah•sah ah•dah kə•sah•lah•hahn*
I'll pay in cash/by credit card.	**Saya bayar kontan/pakai kartu kredit.** *sah•yah bah•yahr kon•tahn/pah•kye kar•too kre•dit*

Renting

I reserved an apartment/a room.	**Saya sudah pesan apartemen/kamar.** *sah•yah soo•dah pə•sahn ah•par•tə•men/kah•mar*
My name is…	**Nama saya…** *nah•mah sah•yah*
Can I have the key/key card?	**Boleh minta kunci/kartu kunci?** *boh•leh min•tah koon•chee/kar•too koon•chee*
Are there…?	**Apakah ada…?** *ah•pah•kah ah•dah*

dishes	**piring** *pee•ring*
pillows	**bantal** *bahn•tahl*
sheets	**seprei** *sə•pray*
towels	**handuk** *hahn•dook*
utensils	**perkakas** *pər•kah•kahs*
When do I put out the bins/recycling?	**Kapan saya harus membuang sampah/ daur-ulang?** *kah•pahn sah•yah hah•roos məm•boo•wahng sahm•pah/dah•woor•oo•lahng*
The…is broken.	**…rusak.** *roo•sahk*
How does the… work?	**Bagaimana cara kerja …?** *bah•gai•mah•nah cha•rah khər•jaa…*
air conditioner	**AC** *ah•seh*
dishwasher	**mesin cuci piring** *mə•sin choo•chee pee•ring*
freezer	**freezer** *freezer*
heater	**pemanas** *pə•mah•nahs*
microwave	**microwave** *microwave*
refrigerator	**lemari es** *lə•mah•ree es*
stove	**kompor gas** *kom•por gas*
washing machine	**mesin cuci** *mə•sin choo•chee*

Domestic Items

I need...	**Saya perlu...** *sah·yah pər·loo*
an adapter	**adaptor** *ah·dahp·tor*
aluminum foil	**kertas timah aluminum** *kər·tahs tee·mah ah·loo·mee·noom*
a bottle opener	**pembuka botol** *pəm·boo·kah boh·tol*
a broom	**sapu** *sah·poo*
a can opener	**pembuka kaleng** *pəm·boo·kah kah·leng*
cleaning supplies	**perlengkapan pembersih** *pər·ləng·kah·pahn pəm·bər·sih*
a corkscrew	**pencungkil tutup gabus** *pən·choong·keel too·toop gah·boos*
detergent	**deterjen** *deh·tər·jen*
dishwashing liquid	**sabun cair pencuci piring** *sah·boon chah·yeer pen·choo·chee pee·ring*
bin bags	**kantung sampah** *kahn·toong sahm·pah*
a lightbulb	**bohlam** *boh·lahm*
matches	**korek api** *koh·rek ah·pee*
a mop	**alat pel** *ah·laht pel*
napkins	**serbet kertas** *sər·bet kər·tahs*
paper towels	**handuk kertas** *hahn·dook kər·tahs*
plastic wrap [cling film]	**pembungkus plastik** *pəm·boong·koos plah·stick*
a plunger	**penyedot wc** *pə·nyə·dot weh·seh*
scissors	**gunting** *goon·ting*
a vacuum cleaner	**penyedot debu** *pə·nyə·dot də·boo*

For In the Kitchen, see page 81.

For Oven Temperatures, see page 175.

Indonesia does not have an extensive network of youth hostels, but the few available are adequate and clean. There are various hostels found in the major cities and tourist destinations such as Jakarta and Bali. The only YMCA can be found in Jakarta. Besides that, budget hotels styled after the bed-and-breakfast concept are also available along Jalan Jaksa in Jakarta, as well as in Bali and Yogyakarta. It is also possible to rent a room from a local family.

At the Hostel

Is there a bed available?	**Ada tempat tidur kosong?** *ah·dah təm·paht tee·door koh·song*
Can I have…?	**Boleh saya minta…?** *boh·leh sah·yah min·tah*
a single/double room	**kamar untuk satu/dua orang** *kah·mar oon·took sah·too/doo·wah oh·rahng*
a blanket	**selimut** *sə·lee·moot*
a pillow	**bantal** *bahn·tahl*
sheets	**seprei** *sə·pray*
a towel	**handuk** *hahn·dook*
Do you have lockers?	**Anda punya lemari?** *ahn·dah poo·nyah lə·mah·ree*
When do you lock up?	**Kapan anda tutup?** *kah·pahn ahn·dah too·toop*
Do I need a membership card?	**Apakah saya perlu kartu anggota?** *ah·pah·kah sah·yah pər·loo kar·too ahng·goh·tah*
Here's my International Student Card.	**Ini Kartu Pelajar Internasional saya.** *ee·nee kar·too pə·lah·jar In·tər·nah·shoh·nahl sah·yah*

There is no organized system for campers but campsites are available within major nature parks like Bumi Perkemahan Cibubur. You will have to pay a fee to pitch your tent there.

YOU MAY SEE…

AIR MINUM *ah•yeer mee•noom*	drinking water
DILARANG BERKEMAH	no camping
dee•lah•rahng bər•keh•mah	
DILARANG MEMBAKAR/MEMANGGANG	no fires/barbecues
dee•lah•rahng mam•bah•kar/mə•mahng•gahng	

Going Camping

Can I camp here?	**Boleh saya berkemah di sini?** *boh•leh sah•yah bər•keh•mah dee see•nee*
Where's the campsite?	**Lokasi kemah di mana?** *loh•kah•see keh•mah dee mah•nah*
What is the charge per day/week?	**Berapa biayanya per hari/minggu?** *bə•rah•pah bee•yah•yah•nyah pər hah•ree/ming•goo*
Are there…?	**Apakah ada…?** *ah•pah•kah ah•dah*
cooking facilities	**perlengkapan memasak** *pər•ləng•kah•pahn mə•mah•sahk*
electric outlets	**soket listrik** *soh•ket lis•trik*
laundry facilities	**fasilitas laundry** *fah•see•lee•tahs laundry*
showers	**shower** *shower*
tents for hire	**penyewaan tenda** *pə•nye•wah•ahn ten•dah*
Where can I empty the chemical toilet?	**Di mana saya bisa mengosongkan toilet kimia?** *dee mah•nah sah•yah bee•sah mə•ngoh•sohng•kahn toh•ee•leht kee•mee•ah*

Communications

ESSENTIAL

Where's an internet cafe [cyber cafe]?	**Warnet [warung internet] di mana?** *wahr·net [wahr·roong in·tər·net] dee mah·nah*
Can I access the internet/check e-mail?	**Dapatkah saya mengakses internet/ periksa e-mail?** *dah·paht·kah sah·yah mə·ngahk·ses in·tər·net/pə·reek·sah e-mail*
How much per (half) hour?	**Berapa biayanya per (setengah) jam?** *bə·rah·pah bee·yah·yah·nyah pər (sə·tə·ngah) jahm*
How do I connect/ log on?	**Bagaimana cara saya menghubung/log on?** *bah·gye·mah·nah chah·rah sah·yah meng·hu·bhung/ log on*
A phone card, please.	**Minta kartu telepon.** *min·tah kar·too tə·lə·pon*
Can I have your phone number?	**Boleh minta nomor telepon Anda?** *boh·leh min·tah noh·mor tə·lə·pon ahn·dah*
Here's my number/ e-mail.	**Ini nomor/e-mail saya.** *ee·nee noh·mor/e·mail sah·yah*
Call/E-mail me.	**Telepon/E-mail saya.** *tə·lə·pon/e·mail sah·yah*
Hello. This is…	**Halo. Ini…** *hah·loh. ee·nee*
Can I speak to…?	**Bisa bicara dengan…?** *bee·sah bee·chah·rah də·ngahn*
Can you repeat that?	**Bisa diulangi?** *bee·sah dee·oo·lah·ngee*
I'll call back later.	**Saya akan telepon kembali nanti.** *sah·yah ah·kahn tə·lə·pohn kəm·bah·lee nahn·tee*
Bye.	**Bye.** *bye*
Where's the post office?	**Kantor pos di mana?** *kahn·tor pos dee mah·nah*
I'd like to send this to…	**Saya ingin kirim ini ke…** *sah·yah ee·ngin kee·rim ee·nee kə*

Online

Where's an internet cafe?	**Warnet [warung internet] di mana?** *wahr·net [wahr·roong in·tər·net] dee mah·nah*
Does it have wireless internet?	**Punya internet nirkabel?** *poo·nyah internet nir·kah·bəl*
What is the WiFi password?	**Apa kata sandi WiFi-nya?** *ah·pah kah·tah sahn·dee wai·fee·nyah*
Is the WiFi free?	**Apakah WiFi-nya gratis?** *ah·pah·kah wai·fee·nyah grah·tis*
Do you have bluetooth?	**Anda punya Bluetooth?** *ahn·dah poo·nyah bloo·tooth*

Internet-access centers and cafes can be found in major cities in Indonesia. Many hotels offer computer and internet facilities in their business centers, as well as wireless internet access in private rooms, usually for a fee.

YOU MAY SEE...

TUTUP *too•toop*	close
HAPUS *hah•poos*	delete
E-MAIL *e•mail*	e-mail
KELUAR *kə•loo•wahr*	exit
BANTUAN *bahn•too•wahn*	help
PESAN INSTAN *pə•sahn in•stahn*	instant messenger
INTERNET *internet*	internet
LOGIN *log•in*	login
BARU (PESAN) *bah•roo (pə•sahn)*	new (message)
HIDUP/MATI *hee•doop/mah•tee*	on/off
BUKA *boo•kah*	open
CETAK *cheh•tahk*	print
SIMPAN *sim•pahn*	save
KIRIM *kee•rim*	send
NAMA PENGGUNA/ KATA SANDI *nah•mah pəng•goo•nah/ kah•tah sahn•dee*	username/password
INTERNET NIRKABEL *internet nir•kah•bəl*	wireless internet

How do I turn the computer on/off?	**Bagaimana cara menghidupkan/ mematikan komputer?** *bah•gye•mah•nah chah•rah məng•hee•doop•kahn/mə•mah•tee•kahn kom•poo•tər*
Can I...?	**Boleh saya...?** *boh•leh sah•yah*
access the internet	**mengakses internet** *mə•ngahk•ses in•tər•net*
check e-mail	**cek e-mail** *check e-mail*
print	**mencetak** *mən•cheh•tahk*
plug in/charge my laptop/iPhone/ iPad/BlackBerry?	**colokkan/cas laptop/iPhone/iPad/BlackBerry saya?** *choh•lohk•kahn/chahs lahp•tohp/ ai•fohn/ ai•pahd/blehk•beh•ree sah•yah*

access Skype?	**akses Skype?** *ahk·sehs skaip*
use any computer	**menggunakan komputer** *məng·goo·nah·kahn kohm·poo·tar*
How much per (half) hour?	**Berapa biayanya per (setengah) jam?** *bə·rah·pah bee·yah·yah·nyah pər (sə·tə·ngah) jahm*
How do I...?	**Bagaimana cara...?** *bah·gye·mah·nah chah·rah*
connect/ disconnect	**menghubung/memutuskan** *məng·hoo·boong/ mə·moo·toos·kahn*
log on/log off	**menyambung/mematikan** *mə·nyam·bhung/ me·maa·tee·khan*
type this symbol	**mengetik simbol ini** *mə·ngə·tik sim·bol ee·nee*
What's your e-mail?	**Apa email anda?** *ah·pah email ahn·dah*
My e-mail is...	**E-mail saya...** *e·mail sah·yah*
Do you have a scanner?	**Anda punya pemindai?** *ahn·dah poo·nyah pə·meen·dai*

Social Media

Are you on Facebook/ Twitter?	**Anda ada di Facebook/Twitter?** *ahn·dah ah·dah di fehs·book/tweet·tər*
What's your user name?	**Apa nama pengguna Anda?** *ah·pah nah·mah pəng·goo·nah ahn·dah*
I'll add you as a friend.	**Saya akan tambahkan Anda sebagai teman.** *sah·yah ah·kahn tahm·bah·kahn ahn·dah sə·bah·gai tə·mahn*
I'll follow you on Twitter.	**Saya akan mengikuti Twitter Anda.** *sah·yah ah·kan məng·i·koot·ee tweet·tər ahn·dah*
Are you following...?	**Anda mengikuti...?** *ahn·dah məng·i·koot·ee*
I'll put the pictures on Facebook/Twitter.	**Saya akan memasang foto di Facebook/Twitter.** *sah·yah ah·kahn mə·mah·sahng foh·toh dee fehs·book/tweet·tər*

| I'll tag you in the pictures. | **Saya akan menandai Anda di foto-foto itu.** |
| | *Sah•yah ah•kahn mə•nahn•dah•ee Ahn•dah dee foh•toh foh•toh ee•too* |

Phone

A phone card/ prepaid phone card, please.	**Minta kartu telepon/kartu telepon prabayar.**
	min•tah kar•too tə•lə•pon/kar•too tə•lə•pon prah•bah•yar
An international phonecard for…	**Kartu telepon internasional untuk…**
	kar•too tə•lə•pohn in•tər•nah•shoh•nahl oon•took
Australia	**Australia** *os•trah•lee•yah*
Canada	**Kanada** *kah•nah•dah*
Ireland	**Irlandia** *ir•lahn•dee•yah*
the U.K.	**Inggris** *ing•grees*
the U.S.	**A.S.** *ah•es*
How much?	**Berapa?** *bə•rah•pah*
Can I recharge/top up the card for this phone?	**Boleh saya isi ulang/tambah dana kartu untuk telepon ini?** *boh•leh sah•yah ee•see oo•lahng/ tahm•bah dah•nah kar•too oon•took tə•lə•pon ee•nee*
Where's the pay phone?	**Di manakah telepon umum?**
	dee mah•nah•kahteh•leh•pohn oohm•moom

Coin and card operated public phones and **wartels** can be found in most cities in Indonesia. Wartel (**warung telekomunikasi**) refers to a private shop that offers public phones on its premises for use. They are very common throughout Indonesia and can be found on the streets of most cities. Some **wartels** are mobile, taking the form of a vehicle with phones installed. For those who need to go online, there is also '**warnet**' similar to '**wartel**' but providing computers with internet connection.

Prepaid mobile phone cards are also available which you may be able to use with your cellphone to make local and international calls. The main telecommunication operators and network providers in Indonesia are **Telkomsel**, **Pro XL**, and **Indosat**.

Second-hand mobiles phones are also very common, with used phones available for purchase at very reasonable prices.

What's the area/country code for...?	**Berapa kode area/negara untuk...?** *bə·rah·pah koh·də ah·reh·yah/nə·gah·rah oon·took*
What's the number for Information?	**Berapa nomor untuk informasi?** *bə·rah·pah noh·mor oon·took in·for·mah·see*
I'd like the number for...	**Saya perlu nomor telepon untuk...** *sah·yah pər·loo noh·mor tə·lə·pon oon·took*
I'd like to call collect [reverse the charges].	**Saya ingin menelepon collect.** *sah·yah ee·ngin mə·nə·lə·pon collect*
My phone doesn't work here.	**Telepon saya tidak berfungsi di sini.** *tə·lə·pon sah·yah tee·dahk ber·foong·see dee see·nee*
What network are you on?	**Apa jaringan telepon Anda?** *ah·pah jah·reeng·ahn teh·leh·pohn ahn·dah*

YOU MAY HEAR...

Siapa yang menelepon?
see·yah·pah yahng mə·nə·lə·pon
Who's calling?

Tunggu sebentar. *toong·goo sə·ben·tar*
Hold on.

Saya akan sambungkan.
sah·yah ah·kahn sahm·boong·kahn
I'll put you through.

Dia tidak ada di sini/sedang
menelepon. *dee·yah tee·dahk ah·dah*
dee see·nee/sə·dahng mə·nə·lə·pon
He/She is not here/
on another line.

Anda ingin meninggalkan pesan?
ahn·dah ee·ngin mə·ning·gahl·kahn pə·sahn
Would you like to leave
a message?

Telepon kembali nanti/ 10 menit lagi.
tə·lə·pon kəm·bah·lee nahn·tee/
sə·poo·looh mə·nit lah·gee
Call back later/
in 10 minutes.

Bolehkah dia menelepon Anda kembali?
boh·leh·kah dee·yah mə·nə·lə·pon ahn·dah
kəm·bah·lee
Can he/she call you back?

Berapa nomor anda? *bə·rah·pah*
noh·mor ahn·dah
What's your number?

Is it 3G?	**Apakah 3G?** *ah·pah·kah tree·jee*
I have run out of credit/minutes.	**Saya kehabisan pulsa.** *sah·yah kə·hah·bees·ahn pool·sah*
Can I buy some credit?	**Bisakah saya membeli pulsa?** *bee·sah·kah sah·yah məm·bə·lee pool·sah*
Do you have a phone charger?	**Apakah Anda punya pengecas telepon?** *ah·pah·kah ahn·dah poo·nyah pə·ngə·chahs teh·leh·pohn*

To call Indonesia (when overseas), dial: +62 + city area code + phone number.
For calls within Indonesia, dial 0 + area code + the phone number.
For calls to the U.S. or Canada (from Indonesia), dial 00 + 1 + area code + phone number.
For calls to the U.K. (from Indonesia), dial 00 + 44 + area code + phone number.

Can I have your number?	**Boleh minta nomor telepon anda?** *boh·leh min·tah noh·mor tə·lə·pon ahn·dah*
Here's my number.	**Ini nomor saya.** *ee·nee noh·mor sah·yah*
Please call me.	**Tolong telepon saya.** *toh·lohng tə·lə·pon sah·yah.*
Please text me.	**Tolong kirim SMS ke saya.** *toh·lohng kee·rim sms kə sah·yah.*
I'll call you.	**Saya akan menelepon anda.** *sah·yah ah·kahn mə·nə·lə·pon ahn·dah*
I'll text you.	**Saya akan SMS anda.** *sah·yah ah·kahn sms ahn·dah.*

Telephone Etiquette

Hello. This is…	**Halo. Ini…** *hah·loh. ee·nee*
Can I speak to…?	**Bisa bicara dengan…?** *bee·sah bee·chah·rah də·ngahn*
Extension…	**Nomor pesawat…** *noh·mor pə·sah·waht*
Speak louder/more slowly, please.	**Tolong bicara lebih keras/agak perlahan.** *toh·lohng bee·chah·rah lə·beeh kə·rahs/ ah·gahk pər·lah·hahn*
Can you repeat that?	**Bisa diulangi?** *bee·sah dee·oo·lah·ngee*
I'll call back later.	**Saya akan telepon kembali nanti.** *sah·yah ah·kahn tə·lə·pohn kəm·bah·lee nahn·tee*
Bye.	**Bye.** *bye*

For Numbers, see page 169.

Fax

Can I send/receive a fax here?	**Dapatkah saya mengirim/ menerima faks disini?** *dah·paht·kah sah·yah mə·ngee·rim/ mə·nə·ree·mah feks dee·see·nee*
What's the fax number (here)?	**Berapa nomor faks disini?** *bə·rah·pah noh·mor feks dee·see·nee*
Please fax this to…	**Tolong faks ini ke…** *toh·long feks ee·nee kə*

Post

Where's the post office/mailbox [postbox]?	**Kantor pos/kotak pos di mana?** *kahn·tor pos/koh·tahk pos dee mah·nah*
A stamp for this postcard/letter to…	**Perangko untuk kartu pos/surat ini ke…** *pə·rahng·koh oon·took kar·too pos/soo·raht ee·nee kə*
How much?	**Berapa?** *bə·rah·pah*

Post offices can be found throughout Indonesia. They normally provide express, registered and general mail services. At major post offices, you can use the Expedited Mail Service (EMS) for international/overseas delivery.

YOU MAY HEAR...

Isi formulir laporan pabean. *ee·see for·moo·leer lah·poh·rahn pah·be·yahn*

Fill out the customs declaration form.

Berapa nilainya? *bə·rah·pah nee·lye·nyah*

What's the value?

Ada apa di dalamnya? *aa·daa aa·paa dee·dha·laam·nyah*

What's inside?

Send this package by airmail/express	**Kirim paket ini lewat pos udara/kilat** *kee·rim pah·ket ee·nee leh·waht pos oo·dah·rah/ kee·laht*
A receipt, please.	**Tolong tanda terimanya.** *tho·long tahn·dah tə·ree·mah·nyah*

Food & Drink

ESSENTIAL

Can you recommend a good restaurant/bar?	**Bisakah anda menyarankan restoran/bar yang bagus?** *bee·sah·kah ahn·dah mə·nyah·rahn·kahn res·toh·rahn/bar yahng bah·goos*
Is there an Indonesian/inexpensive restaurant nearby?	**Apakah ada restoran Indonesia/tidak mahal di sekitar sini?** *ah·pah·kah ahn·dah res·toh·rahn in·doh·neh·shah/tee·dahk mah·hahl dee sə·kee·tahr see·nee*
A table for..., please.	**Tolong meja untuk...** *toh·lohng meh·jah oon·took*
Can we sit...?	**Bisa kami duduk...?** *bee·sah kah·mee doo·dook*
here/there	**di sini/di sana** *dee see·nee/dee sah·nah*
outside	**di luar** *dee loo·wahr*
in a non-smoking area	**di area tidak merokok** *dee ah·reh·yah tee·dahk mə·roh·kohk*
I'm waiting for someone.	**Saya menunggu seseorang.** *sah·yah mə·noong·goo sə·sə·oh·rahng*
Where's the restroom [toilet]?	**Kamar kecil di mana?** *kah·mar kə·cheel dee·mah·nah*
A menu, please.	**Tolong minta menunya.** *toh·long min·tah meh·noo·nyah*
What do you recommend?	**Apa yang anda sarankan?** *ah·pah yahng ahn·dah sah·rahn·kahn*
I'd like...	**Saya mau...** *sah·yah mah·woo*
Some more..., please.	**Tolong tambah lagi...** *toh·long tahm·bah lah·gee*

Enjoy your meal!	**Selamat makan!**
	sə·lah·maht mah·kahn
The check [bill], please.	**Tolong minta bonnya.**
	toh·long min·tah bon·nyah
Is service included?	**Apakah sudah termasuk pelayanan?**
	ah·pah·kah soo·dah tər·mah·sook pə·lah·yah·nahn
Can I pay by credit card/have a receipt?	**Boleh saya bayar dengan kartu kredit/ minta kwitansi?**
	boh·leh sah·yah bah·yahr də·ngahn kahr·too kre·dit/min·tah quee·tahn·see
Thank you!	**Terima kasih!** *tə·ree·mah kah·seeh*

Where to Eat

Can you recommend…?	**Bisakah Anda menyarankan…?**
	bee·sah·kah ahn·dah mə·nyah·rahn·kahn
a restaurant	**restoran** *res·toh·rahn*
a bar	**bar** *bar*
a cafe	**kafe** *kah·feh*
a fast-food restaurant	**restoran cepat-saji** *res·toh·rahn cə·paht·sah·jee*
a cheap restaurant	**restoran murah** *rehs·toh·rahn moo·rah*
an expensive restaurant	**restoran mahal** *rehs·toh·rahn mah·hahl*
a restaurant with a good view	**restoran berpemandangan indah** *rehs·toh·rahn bher·pə·mahn·dahng·ahn een·dah*
an authentic/non-touristy restaurant	**Restoran non-turis/autentik** *rehs·toh·rahn nohn·too·rees/ow·tehn·tik*
a snack bar	**snack bar** *snack bar*
a coffee shop	**coffee shop** *coffee shop*
a hawker centre	**pusat kakilim** *poo·saht kah·kee·lee·mah*

In the big cities, restaurants serving a wide variety of international cuisine can be found. Halal food is widely available as Indonesia is a predominantly Muslim country. Vegetarians may face some difficulties, as it can be hard to find strictly vegetarian dishes. Vegetables are often prepared with condiments or other ingredients which may contain products of animal-origin.

Reservations & Preferences

I'd like to reserve a table...	**Saya ingin pesan tempat...** *sah•yah ee•ngin pə•sahn təm•paht*
for two	**untuk dua orang** *oon•took doo•wah oh•rahng*
for this evening	**untuk malam ini** *oon•took mah•lahm ee•nee*
for tomorrow at...	**untuk besok jam...** *oon•took beh•sok jahm*
A table for two, please.	**Tolong meja untuk dua orang.** *toh•lohng meh•jah oon•took doo•wah oh•rahng*
We have a reservation.	**Kami sudah pesan tempat.** *kah•mee soo•dah pə•sahn təm•paht*
My name is...	**Nama saya...** *nah•mah sah•yah*

It is the local custom in Indonesia to eat with your hands, i.e. without using utensils. The right hand is used to pick up food and eat. The left is used to take food from communal plates using utensils. It is taboo to pick up food using either hand directly from the communal plates — always use the utensils provided.

Food stalls and hawker centers are popular with the locals, and they usually serve meals all day long. You'll often find open-air food stalls lining both sides of a street offering dishes with seafood, chicken, vegetables, barbecued meat, soup, noodles or rice. Tables and/or seating are often available, or you can eat standing.

Can we sit…?	**Bisa kami duduk…?** *bee·sah kah·mee doo·dook*
here/there	**disini/disana** *dee see·nee/dee sah·nah*
outside	**di luar** *dee loo·wahr*
in a non-smoking area	**di area tidak merokok** *dee ah·reh·yah tee·dahk mə·roh·kok*
by the window	**dekat jendela** *də·kaht jən·de·lah*
Where's the restroom [toilet]?	**Kamar kecil di mana?** *kah·mar kə·cheel dee·mah·nah*

How to Order

Waiter/Waitress!	**Mas/Mbak!** *mahs/mbahk*
We're ready to order (food).	**Kami mau pesan sekarang.** *kah·mee mah·woo pə·sahn sə·kah·rahng*
The wine list, please.	**Tolong minta daftar anggur.** *toh·lohng min·tah dahf·tar ahng·goor*
I'd like…	**Saya mau…** *sah·yah mah·woo*
a bottle of…	**sebotol…** *sə·boh·tol*

YOU MAY HEAR...

Anda sudah pesan tempat?
ahn·dah soo·dah pə·sahn təm·paht

Do you have a reservation?

Berapa orang? *bə·rah·pah oh·rahng*

How many (people)?

Merokok atau tidak merokok?
mə·roh·kok ah·tow tee·dahk mə·roh·kok

Smoking or non-smoking?

Mau pesan sekarang?
mah·woo pə·sahn sə·kah·rahng

Are you ready to order (food)?

Anda ingin pesan apa?
ahn·dah ee·ngin pə·sahn ah·pah

What would you like?

Saya menyarankan... *sah·yah mə·nyah·rahn·kahn*

I recommend...

Selamat makan. *sə·lah·maht mah·kahn*

Enjoy your meal.

a carafe of...	**satu picer...** *sah·too pee·cer*
a glass of...	**segelas...** *sə·gə·lahs*
The menu, please.	**Tolong minta menunya.** *toh·lohng min·tah meh·noo·nyah*

Do you have…?	**Anda punya…?** *ahn·dah poo·nyah*	
a menu in English	**menu dalam bahasa Inggris** *meh·noo dah·lahm bah·hah·sah ing·grees*	
a fixed-price menu	**menu dengan daftar harga** *meh·noo də·ngahn dahf·tar har·gah*	
a children's menu	**menu untuk anak kecil** *meh·noo oon·took ah·nahk kə·cheel*	
What do you recommend?	**Apa yang anda sarankan?** *ah·pah yahng ahn·dah sah·rahn·kahn*	
What's this?	**Apa ini?** *ah·pah ee·nee*	
What's in it?	**Isinya apa?** *ee·see·nyah ah·pah*	
Is it spicy?	**Apakah pedas?** *ah·pah·kah phe·das*	
I'd like…	**Saya mau…** *sah·yah mah·woo*	
More…, please.	**Tolong tambah lagi…** *toh·long tahm·bah lah·gee*	
With/Without…, please.	**Tolong, pakai/tanpa…** *toh·lohng, pah·kye/ tahn·pah*	
I can't have…	**Saya tidak boleh makan…** *sah·yah tee·dahk boh·leh mah·kahn*	
rare	**agak mentah** *ah·gahk mən·tah*	
medium	**setengah matang** *sə·tə·ngah mah·tahng*	
well-done	**matang** *mah·tahng*	
Without…, please.	**Tolong, tanpa…** *toh·lohng, tahn·pah*	
It's to go [take away].	**Untuk dibungkus.** *oon·took dee·boong·koos*	

For Drinks, see page 82.

Cooking Methods

baked	**dipanggang** *dee·pahng·gahng*
boiled	**direbus** *dee·rə·boos*
braised	**dikukus** *dee·koo·koos*
breaded	**dibalut tepung roti** *dee·bah·loot tə·poong ro·tee*
creamed	**diberi krim** *dee·bə·ree krim*

YOU MAY SEE...

HARGA PASTI *har-gah pahs-tee*	fixed-price
MENU HARI INI *meh-noo hah-ree ee-nee*	menu of the day
HIDANGAN PENDAMPING	side dishes
hee-dah-ngahn pən-dahm-ping	
SPESIAL *spe-shahl*	specials
TAK TERMASUK LAYANAN	service not included
tahk tər-mah-sook lah-yahn-ahn	
BIAYA MASUK *bhe-a-ya mha-shook*	cover charge

diced	**diiris dadu** *dee-ee-riss dah-doo*	
fileted	**dibuang tulang** *dee-boo-wahng too-lahng*	
fried	**digoreng** *dee-go-reng*	
grilled	**dibakar** *dee-bah-kar*	
poached	**dimasak tanpa kulit** *dee-mah-sak tahn-pah koo-lit*	
roasted	**dipanggang** *dee-pahng-gahng*	
sautéed	**ditumis** *dee-too-miss*	
smoked	**diasap** *dee-ah-sahp*	
steamed	**dikukus** *dee-koo-koos*	
stewed	**direbus dengan api kecil** *dee-rə-boos də-ngahn*	
	ah-pee kə-cheel	
stuffed	**diisi** *dee-ee-see*	

Dietary Requirements

I'm...	**Saya...** *sah-yah*	
diabetic	**diabetis** *dee-yah-be-tiss*	
lactose intolerant	**tidak tahan gula** *tee-dahk tah-hahn goo-lah*	
vegetarian	**vegetarian** *veh-geh-tah-ree-yahn*	
I'm allergic to...	**Saya alergi terhadap...** *sah-yah ah-ler-gee*	
	tər-hahn-dahp	

I can't eat…	**Saya tidak bisa makan…** *sah•yah tee•dahk bee•sah mah•kahn*
dairy	**produk susu** *pro•dook soo•soo*
gluten	**ketan** *kə•tahn*
nuts	**kacang** *kah•chahng*
pork	**babi** *bah•bee*
shellfish	**kerang** *kə•rahng*
spicy foods	**makanan pedas** *mah•kah•nahn phe•das*
wheat	**gandum** *gahn•doom*
Is it halal/cocher?	**Apakah halal?** *ah•pah•kah hah•lahl*
Do you have…?	**Anda punya…?** *ahn•dah poo•nyah*
skimmed milk	**susu skim** *soo•soo skeem*
whole milk	**susu penuh** *soo•soo pə•nooh*
soya milk	**susu kedelai** *soo•soo kə•də•lai*

Dining with Children

Do you have children's portions?	**Ada porsi untuk anak kecil?** *ahn•dah por•see oon•took ah•nahk kə•cheel*
A highchair/child's seat, please.	**Tolong minta kursi tinggi/kursi anak kecil.** *toh•lohng min•tah koor•see ting•gee/koor•see ah•nahk kə•cheel*

Where can I feed the baby?	**Di mana saya bisa menyusui bayi?** *dee·mah·nah sah·yah bee·sah mə·nyoo·soo·wee bah·yee*
Where can I change the baby?	**Di mana saya bisa mengganti popok bayi?** *dee·mah·nah sah·yah bee·sah məng·gahn·tee po·pok bah·yee*
Can you warm this?	**Bisa tolong hangatkan ini?** *bee·sah toh·lohng hah·ngaht·kahn ee·nee*

How to Complain

How much longer will our food be?	**Berapa lama pesanan kami akan selesai?** *bə·rah·pah lah·mah pə·sah·nahn kah·mee ah·kahn sə·lə·sye*
We can't wait any longer.	**Kami tidak bisa tunggu lebih lama lagi.** *kah·mee tee·dahk bee·sah toong·goo lə·beeh lah·mah lah·gee*
We're leaving (this place).	**Kami akan pergi (meninggalkan tempat ini).** *kah·mee ah·kahn pər·gee (mə·nhing·ghal·kahn tem·phat ee·nee)*
I didn't order this (food).	**Saya tidak memesan ini.** *sah·yah tee·dahk mə·mə·sahn ee·nee*
I ordered...	**Saya memesan...** *sah·yah mə·mə·sahn*
I can't eat this (food).	**Saya tidak bisa makan ini.** *sah·yah tee·dahk bee·sah mah·kahn ee·nee*
This (food) is too...	**Makanan ini terlalu...** *mah·kah·nahn ee·nee tər·lah·loo*
cold/hot	**dingin/panas** *dee·ngin/pah·nahs*
salty/spicy	**asin/pedas** *ah·sin/phe·das*
tough/bland	**alot/hambar** *ah·lot/hahm·bar*
This isn't clean/ fresh.	**Ini tidak bersih/segar.** *ee·nee tee·dahk bər·seeh/sə·gar*

In major hotels, an 11% government tax and 11% service charge is added to the bill, so tipping is not obligatory. However, at the major tourist spots, tipping is quite common. In some restaurants, a 5 to 10% service charge is added to the bill. In this case, you can just leave behind the loose change. Otherwise, a simple 'thank you' ('**terima kasih**') and a smile will do. If no service charge is added, you can offer a tip of between IDR5,000 to 10% of the total bill. Take note that tourist guides do expect to receive a tip.

Paying

The check [bill], please.	**Tolong minta bonnya.** *toh•lohng min•tah bon•nyah*
Separate checks [bills], please.	**Tolong minta bonnya dipisah.** *toh•lohng min•tah bon•nyah dee•pee•sah*
It's all together.	**Semua digabung.** *sə•moo•wah dee•gha•bhung*
Is service included?	**Apakah sudah termasuk pelayanan?** *ah•pah•kah soo•dah tər•mah•sook pə•lah•yah•nahn*
What's this amount for?	**Jumlah ini untuk apa?** *joom•lah ee•nee oon•took ah•pah*
I didn't eat/drink... I ate/drank...	**Saya tidak makan/minum itu. Saya makan/minum...** *sah•yah tee•dahk mah•kahn/mee•noom ee•too. sah•yah mah•kahn/mee•noom*
Can I have a receipt/ an itemized bill?	**Bisa minta kwitansi/perincian bon?** *bee•sah min•tah quee•tahn•see/pə•rin•chee•yahn bon*
That was delicious!	**Enak sekali!** *eh•nahk sə•kah•lee*
I've already paid.	**Saya sudah membayar.** *Sah•yah soo•dah məm•bah•yahr*

Meals & Cooking

Breakfast

bacon	**daging bacon** *dah•geeing bacon*
bread	**roti** *roh•tee*
butter	**mentega** *mən•teh•gah*
cereal	**sereal** *seh•reh•yahl*
cheese	**keju** *keh•joo*
coffee/tea…	**kopi/teh…** *koh•pee/teh*
black	**hitam** *hee•tahm*
decaf	**decaf** *decaf*
with milk	**pakai susu** *pah•kye soo•soo*
with sugar	**pakai gula** *pah•kye goo•lah*
with artificial	**pakai gula buatan**
sweetener	*pah•kye goo•lah boo•wah•tahn*
egg, fried	**telur, goreng** *tə•loor, goh•reng*
egg, hard-/soft-	**telur rebus matang/setengah matang**
boiled	*tə•loor rə•boos mah•tahng/sə•tə•ngah mah•tahng*
jam/jelly	**selai/jeli** *sə•lye/jeh•lee*
…juice	**jus…** *joos…*
apple	**apel** *ah•pəl*

watermelon	**semangka** sə·mahng·kah
orange	**jeruk** jə·rook
milk	**susu** soo·soo
oatmeal	**bubur gandum** boo·boor ghan·dhum
omelet	**telur dadar** tə·loor dahn·dahr
sausage	**sosis** so·sees
toast	**roti panggang** roh·tee pang·ghang
yogurt	**yogurt** yogurt
water	**air** ah·yeer

Appetizers

...soup	**sup...** soop
chicken	**ayam** ah·yahm
meat, seafood	**daging, seafood dan telur** dah·ging, seafood
and egg	dahn tə·loor
pork	**babi** bah·bee
lamb	**kambing** kahm·bing
oxtail	**buntut sapi** boon·toot sah·pee
seafood	**seafood** seafood
spare rib	**tulang iga** too·lahng ee·gah
squid	**cumi** choo·mee
tomato	**tomat** to·maht
vegetable	**sayuran** sah·yoo·rahn

Fish & Seafood

carp	**kerapu** kə·rah·poo
clam	**kerang** kə·rahng
cod	**cod** cod
crab	**kepiting** kə·pee·ting
halibut	**ikan pecak** ee·kahn pe·chahk
herring	**haring** hah·reeng
lobster	**lobster** lobster

octopus	**gurita**	goo·ree·tah
oyster	**tiram**	tee·rahm
salmon	**salmon**	sahl·mon
salted fish	**ikan asin**	ee·kahn ah·sin
sea bass	**bas laut**	bahs lah·woot
shrimp	**udang**	oo·dahng
sole	**ikan tapak kaki**	ee·kahn tah·pahk kah·kee
squid	**cumi**	choo·mee
swordfish	**ikan cucut**	ee·kahn choo·choot
trout	**trout**	trout
tuna	**tuna**	tuna

Meat & Poultry

barbecued pork	**babi panggang**	bah·bee pahng·gahng
beef	**sapi**	sah·pee
chicken	**ayam**	ah·yahm
duck	**bebek**	beh·bek
ham	**ham**	hahm
lamb	**kambing**	kahm·bing
liver	**hati**	hah·tee
oxen entrails	**jerohan sapi**	jə·ro·wahn sah·pee

The majority of Indonesians are Muslims, so it is useful to understand a central part of their eating culture. There are 'halal' and 'non-halal' foods. Halal food means food that is allowed by Muslim law.

pork	**babi**	*bah·bee*
sausage	**sosis**	*so·sees*
spare ribs	**tulang iga**	*too·lahng ee·gah*
steak	**steak**	*steak*
veal	**anak sapi**	*ah·nahk sah·pee*
oxen tripe	**babat sapi**	*bah·baht sah·pee*

Vegetables & Staples

asparagus	**asparagus**	*ahs·pah·rah·goos*
broccoli	**brokoli**	*bro·ko·lee*
cabbage	**kol**	*kol*
capsicum	**paprika**	*paprika*
carrot	**wortel**	*wor·təl*
cauliflower	**kembang kol**	*kəm·bahng kol*
celery	**seledri**	*sə·le·dree*
Chinese cabbage	**sawi putih**	*sah·wee poo·teeh*
corn	**jagung**	*jah·goong*
curry leaves	**daun kari**	*dah·woon kah·ree*
long bean	**kacang panjang**	*kah·chahng pahn·jahng*
eggplant [aubergine]	**terong**	*teh·rong*
garlic	**bawang putih**	*bah·wahng poo·teeh*
green bean	**buncis**	*boon·chis*
lemongrass	**sereh**	*sə·reh*
lettuce	**selada**	*sə·lahn·dah*
mushroom	**jamur**	*jah·moor*

olive	**zaitun** *zye·toon*
okra [lady's finger]	**okra** *ok·rah*
scallion [spring onion]	**daun bawang** *dah·woon bah·wahng*
noodles	**mie** *mee*
pea	**ercis** *er·chis*
potato	**kentang** *kən·tahng*
radish	**lobak** *loh·bhak*
rice	**beras** *bə·rahs*
red/green pepper	**paprika merah/hijau** *paprika meh·rah/hee·jow*
seaweed	**rumput laut** *room·put lah·woot*
soy bean	**kedelai** *kə·də·lye*
spinach	**bayam** *bah·yahm*
tofu	**tahu** *tah·hoo*
tomato	**tomat** *to·maht*
vegetable	**sayuran** *sah·yoo·rahn*
zucchini	**zucchini** *zucchini*

Fruit

apple	**apel** *ah·pəl*
banana	**pisang** *pee·sahng*
carambola [starfruit]	**belimbing** *bə·lim·bing*
chiku	**sawo** *sah·woh*
custard apple	**srikaya** *sree·kah·yah*
coconut	**kelapa** *kə·lah·pah*
dates	**kurma** *koor·mah*
mandarin orange	**jeruk mandarin** *jə·rook mahn·dah·rin*
mangosteen	**manggis** *mahng·giss*
fruits	**buah-buahan** *boo·wah·boo·wah·hahn*
grapefruit	**jeruk keprok** *jə·rook kə·prok*
grape	**anggur** *ahng·goor*

jackfruit	**nangka** *nahng·kah*
kiwi fruit	**kiwi** *kee·wee*
lemon	**lemon** *leh·mon*
lime	**jeruk nipis** *ja·rook nee·piss*
mango	**mangga** *mahng·gah*
nutmeg	**buah pala** *boo·wah pah·lah*
orange	**jeruk** *ja·rook*
papaya	**pepaya** *pa·pah·yah*
peach	**peach** *peach*
pear	**pir** *peer*
pineapple	**nanas** *nah·nahs*
plum	**plum** *plum*
pomegranate	**delima** *da·lee·mah*
pomelo	**jeruk bali** *ja·rook bah·lee*
strawberry	**stroberi** *stro·beh·ree*
watermelon	**semangka** *sa·mahng·kah*

Dessert

crushed ice with syrup, condensed milk and kidney beans	**Es Kacang Merah** *es kah·chahng meh·rah*
crushed ice with coconut milk, green jelly, red beans and brown sugar	**Es Cendol** *es cen·doll*
milk curd	**Kue susu** *koo·weh soo·soo*
soy bean curd	**Kue kedelai** *koo·weh ka·da·lye*
mixed fruit	**Buah campur** *boo·wah chahm·poor*
bean paste	**Kue selai kacang** *koo·weh sa·lye kah·chahng*
ice cream	**Es Krim** *es krim*

| cake | **kue** *koo•weh* |
| peanut cake | **kue kacang** *koo•weh kah•chahng* |

Sauces & Condiments

salt	**garam** *gah•rahm*
pepper	**lada** *lah•dah*
mustard	**mustar** *moos•tahr*
ketchup	**saus** *sah•oos*

At the Market

Where are the trolleys/baskets?	**Troli/Keranjangnya di mana?** *tro•lee/kə•rahn•jahng•nyah dee mah•nah*
Where is…?	**…di mana?** *dee•mah•nah*
I'd like some of that/this.	**Saya ingin itu/ini.** *sah•yah ee•ngin ee•too/ee•nee*
Can I taste it?	**Boleh saya cicipi?** *boh•leh sah•yah chee•chee•pee*
I'd like…	**Saya minta…** *sah•yah min•tah*
a kilo/half-kilo of…	**sekilo/setengah kilo…** *sə•kee•lo/sə•tə•ngah kee•loh*
a liter of…	**seliter…** *sə•lee•tər*
a piece of…	**sepotong…** *sə•po•tong*
a slice of…	**seiris…** *sə•ee•riss*

More/Less.	**Tambah/Kurangi.** *tahm·bah/koo·rah·ngee*
How much?	**Berapa?** *bə·rah·pah*
Where do I pay?	**Di mana saya membayar?**
	dee·mah·nah sah·yah məm·bah·yar
A bag, please.	**Tolong minta kantung.**
	toh·lohng min·tah kahn·toong
I'm being helped.	**Saya sedang dibantu.**
	sah·yah sə·dahng dee·bahn·too

YOU MAY SEE…

TANGGAL KEDALUWARSA	expiry date
tahng·gahl kə·dah·loo·wahr·sah	
KALORI *kah·loh·ree*	calories
BEBAS LEMAK *beh·bahs lə·mahk*	fat free
SIMPAN DI LEMARI ES *sim·pahn*	keep refrigerated
dee lə·mah·ree es	
MUNGKIN MENGANDUNG SISA…	may contain traces of…
moong·kin mə·ngahn·doong see·sah	
BISA DIMASAK DENGAN MICROWAVE	microwavable
bee·sah dee·mah·sahk də·ngahn	
mee·kroh·wehf	
DIJUAL OLEH… *dee·joo·wahl oh·leh*	sell by…
COCOK UNTUK VEGETARIAN *cho·chok*	suitable for vegetarians
oon·took veh·geh·tah·ree·yahn	

YOU MAY HEAR…

Ada yang dapat saya bantu? *ahn·dah yahng dah·paht sah·yah bahn·too*   Can I help you?

Anda ingin apa? *ahn·dah ee·ngin ah·pah*   What would you like?

Ada lagi lainnya? *ahn·dah lah·gee lah·yeen·nyah*   Anything else?

Semuanya…Rupiah. *sə·moo·wah·nyah… roo·pee·yah*   That's…Rupiah.

In the Kitchen

bottle opener	**pembuka botol** *pəm·boo·kah boh·tol*
bowl	**mangkuk** *mahng·kook*
can opener	**pembuka kaleng** *pəm·boo·kah kah·leng*
ceramic spoon	**sendok keramik** *sen·dok kə·rah·mik*
corkscrew	**pencungkil tutup gabus** *pən·choong·keel too·toop gah·boos*
clay pot	**periuk tembikar** *pə·ree·yook təm·bee·kar*
cup	**cangkir** *chahng·keer*
fork	**garpu** *gar·poo*
frying pan	**penggorengan** *pəng·goh·reh·ngahn*
glass	**gelas** *gə·lahs*
knife	**pisau** *pee·sow*
grater	**parutan** *pah·roo·tahn*
napkin	**serbet** *sər·bet*
plate	**piring** *pee·ring*
pot	**periuk** *pə·ree·yook*
spatula	**spatula** *spah·too·lah*
spoon	**sendok** *sen·dok*

Drinks

ESSENTIAL

The wine list/drink menu, please.
Tolong minta daftar wine/minuman.
toh·long min·tah dahf·tar wine/mee·noo·mahn

What do you recommend?
Apa yang anda sarankan? *ah·pah yahng ahn·dah sah·rahn·kahn*

I'd like a bottle/glass of red/white wine.
Saya minta sebotol/segelas anggur merah/putih *sah·yah min·tah sə·boh·tol/ sə·gə·lahs ahng·goor meh·rah/poo·teeh*

The house wine, please.
Tolong minta house wine. *toh·long min·tah house wine*

Another bottle/glass, please.
Tolong satu botol/gelas lagi.
toh·long sah·too boh·tol/gə·lahs lah·gee

I'd like a local beer.
Saya ingin bir lokal.
sah·yah ee·ngin beer lo·kahl

Can I buy you a drink?
Bisa saya traktir minum? *bee·sah sah·yah trahk·teer mee·noom*

Cheers!
Cheers! *cheers*

A coffee/tea, please.	**Tolong minta kopi/teh.** *toh‧long min‧tah koh‧pee/teh*
Black.	**Hitam.** *hee‧tahm*
With...	**Pakai...** *pah‧kye*
milk	**susu** *soo‧soo*
sugar	**gula** *goo‧lah*
artificial sweetener	**gula buatan** *goo‧lah boo‧wah‧tahn*
A..., please.	**Tolong minta...** *toh‧lohng min‧tah*
juice	**jus** *joos*
soda	**soda** *soh‧dah*
(sparkling/still) water	**air (sparkling/still)** *ah‧yeer (sparkling/still)*
Is the water safe to drink?	**Apakah air ini aman untuk diminum?** *ah‧paa‧kah ah‧yeer ee‧nee ah‧mahn oon‧took dee‧mee‧noom*

Drinking or using tap water for brushing your teeth is not recommended in Indonesia. Avoid drinks served with ice as well. Most water served in restaurants will be boiled or purified and is safe for consumption. As a precaution, drink boiled water, especially in rural areas. Bottled water and mineral water can be purchased in major towns.

Non-alcoholic Drinks

coffee	**kopi** *ko‧pee*
cola	**kola** *ko‧la*
Chinese tea	**teh China** *teh chee‧nah*
hot chocolate	**cokelat panas** *cho‧kə‧laht pah‧nahs*

YOU MAY HEAR...

Mau minum apa? *mah·woo mee·noom ah·pah* Can I get you a drink?

Pakai susu atau gula? *pah·kye soo·soo* With milk or sugar?
ah·tow goo·lah

Soda atau air? *soh·dah ah·tow ah·eer* Sparkling or still water?

juice	**jus** *joos*	
...tea	**teh...** *teh*	
green	**hijau** *hee·jow*	
iced	**es** *es*	
lemon	**lemon** *leh·mon*	
milk	**susu** *soo·soo*	
barley	**barley** *barley*	
lemonade	**air jeruk** *ah·yeer jə·rook*	
rose syrup with milk	**sirup rose pakai susu** *see·roop rose pah·kye soo·soo*	
milk	**susu** *soo·soo*	
syrup	**sirop** *see·rop*	
soda	**soda** *soh·dah*	
(sparkling/still) water	**air (sparkling/still)** *ah·yeer (sparkling/still)*	
white coffee	**kopi susu** *ko·pee soo·soo*	
yogurt drink	**minuman yogurt** *mee·noo·mahn yogurt*	

Aperitifs, Cocktails & Liqueurs

brandy	**brendi** *brehn·dee*
gin	**gin** *geen*
rum	**rum** *room*
scotch	**scotch** *schohtch*
tequila	**tequila** *teh·qee·lah*

| vodka | **vodka** *vod·kah* |
| whisky | **whisky** *whees·ki* |

Beer

beer	**bir** *beer*
bottled/draft/canned	**botol/draft/kaleng** *boh·tol/draft/kah·leng*
dark/light	**hitam/light** *hee·tam/light*
local/imported	**lokal/impor** *lo·kahl/im·por*
non-alcoholic	**non-alkohol** *nohn·ahl·koh·hohl*

Wine

...wine	**...anggur** *ahng·goor*
red/white	**merah/putih** *meh·rah/poo·tih*
house/table	**rumah/meja** *roo·mah/meh·jah*
dry/sweet	**kering/manis** *kə·reeng/mah·nees*
sparkling	**bersoda** *bər·soh·dah*
champagne	**sampanye** *sahm·pah·nyə*
dessert wine	**anggur pencuci mulut** *ahng·goor pən·choo·chee moo·loot*

Alcohol in Indonesia ranges from inexpensive local beers to more expensive drinks such as imported wine and liquor. Traditional alcoholic drinks such as **tuak** (sugar palm wine consisting of 15% alcohol) and **arak** (distilled **tuak** consisting of 40% alcohol) are also available in local stores, but they may contain impurities due to the distillation methods. Alcohol is forbidden to Muslims, but it is available at pubs, hotels, restaurants and in Chinese eateries, as well as supermarkets in towns and tourist areas.

On the Menu

anchovy	**ikan haring kecil** ee·kahn hah·reeng kə·cheel
aperitif	**aperitif** ah·pə·ree·teef
apple	**apel** ah·pəl
artichoke	**artichoke** artichoke
artificial sweetener	**gula buatan** goo·lah boo·wah·tahn
asparagus	**asparagus** ahs·pah·rah·goos
avocado	**alpukat** ahl·poo·kaht
banana	**pisang** pee·sahng
bass	**bass** bahs
bay leaf	**daun salam** dah·woon sah·lahm
bean	**kacang** kah·chahng
bean sprout	**tauge** toh·geh
beef	**sapi** sah·pee
beer	**bir** beer
brandy	**brandi** brandy
bread	**roti** roh·tee
breast (of chicken)	**dada (ayam)** dahn·dah (ah·yahm)
broth	**kaldu** kahl·doo
butter	**mentega** mən·teh·gah
cabbage	**kol** kol
cake	**kue** koo·weh
candy [sweets]	**permen** pər·men
caramel	**karamel** kah·rah·mel
carrot	**wortel** wor·təl
cashew	**kacang mede** kah·chahng meh·deh
cauliflower	**kembang kol** kəm·bahng kol
celery	**seledri** sə·leh·dree
cereal	**sereal** seh·reh·yahl
cheese	**keju** keh·joo

chestnut	**kacang berangan**	kah·chahng bə·rah·ngahn
chicken	**ayam**	ah·yahm
chickpea	**biji ercis**	bee·jee er·chis
chili pepper [capsicum]	**cabai**	chah·bye
chives	**kucai**	koo·chye
chocolate	**cokelat**	cho·kə·laht
chopped meat	**daging potong**	dah·ging poh·tong
cider	**cuka apel**	choo·kah ah·pəl
cilantro [coriander]	**ketumbar**	kə·toom·bar
cinnamon	**kayu manis**	kah·yoo mah·niss
clam	**kerang**	kə·rahng
clove	**cengkeh**	cəng·keh
coconut	**kelapa**	kə·lah·pah
cod	**cod**	cod
coffee	**kopi**	koh·pee
consommé	**sup bening**	soop bə·ning
cookie	**kue kering**	koo·weh kə·ring
crab	**kepiting**	kə·pee·ting
crabmeat	**daging kepiting**	dah·ging kə·pee·ting
cracker	**keripik**	kə·ree·pick
cream	**krim**	krim

cream, whipped	**krim, kocok** *krim, ko·chok*
cream cheese	**krim keju** *krim keh·joo*
cucumber	**mentimun/ketimun** *mən·tee·moon/keh·tee·moon*
cumin	**jinten** *jin·tən*
curry leaves	**daun kari** *dah·woon kah·ree*
custard	**puding** *poo·ding*
dates	**kurma** *koor·mah*
dessert wine	**dessert wine** *dessert wine*
duck	**bebek** *beh·bek*
dumpling	**roti kukus** *roh·tee koo·koos*
eel	**belut** *bə·loot*
egg	**telur** *tə·loor*
egg yolk/white	**kuning/putih telur** *koo·ning/poo·teeh tə·loor*
eggplant [aubergine]	**terong** *teh·rong*
fennel	**adas** *ahn·dahs*
fig	**buah ara** *boo·wah ah·rah*
fish	**ikan** *ee·kahn*
french fries	**kentang goreng** *kən·tahng goh·reng*
fritter (banana fritter)	**pisang goreng** *pee·sahng goh·reng*
fruit	**buah** *boo·wah*
game	**permainan** *pər·mah·yee·nahn*

garlic	**bawang putih** *bah·wahng poo·teeh*
gherkin	**ketimun acar** *kə·tee·moon ah·chahr*
giblet	**ampela** *ahm·pə·lah*
gin	**gin** *gin*
ginger	**jahe** *jah·he*
goat	**kambing** *kahm·bing*
goat cheese	**keju susu kambing** *keh·joo soo·soo kahm·bing*
goose	**angsa** *ahng·sah*
grapefruit	**jeruk keprok** *jə·rook kə·prok*
grapes	**anggur** *ahng·goor*
green bean	**buncis** *boon·chis*
guava	**jambu batu** *jahm·boo bah·too*
haddock	**ikan haddock** *ee·kahn haddock*
halibut	**ikan pecak** *ee·kahn pe·chahk*
ham	**ham** *ham*
hamburger	**hamburger** *hamburger*
hazelnut	**kacang hazel** *kah·chahng hazel*
hen	**ayam betina** *ah·yahm bə·tee·nah*
herb	**rempah** *rəm·pah*
herring	**haring** *hah·reeng*
honey	**madu** *mah·doo*
hot dog	**hot dog** *hot dog*
hot pepper sauce	**saos cabai** *sah·woss chah·bye*
ice (cube)	**es batu** *es bah·too*
ice cream	**es krim** *es krim*
jam	**selai** *sə·lye*
jelly	**jeli** *jeh·lee*
juice	**jus** *joos*
ketchup	**saos tomat** *sah·woss to·maht*
lamb	**kambing** *kahm·bing*
leek	**daun bawang** *dah·woon bah·wahng*

lemon	**lemon** *lemon*
lemongrass	**sereh** sə•reh
lemonade	**air jeruk** ah•yeer jə•rook
lentil	**lentil** *lentil*
lettuce	**selada** sə•lahn•dah
lime	**jeruk nipis** jə•rook nee•piss
liquor	**minuman keras** mee•noo•mahn kə•rahs
liver	**hati** hah•tee
lobster	**lobster** *lobster*
longan	**lengkeng** leng•kheng
mackerel	**makarel** mah•kə•rell
mandarin orange	**jeruk mandarin** jə•rook mahn•dah•rin
mango	**mangga** mahng•gah
margarine	**margarin** mahr•gah•rin
marmalade	**marmalade** *marmalade*
mayonnaise	**mayones** mah•yoh•ness
meat	**daging** dah•ging
milk	**susu** soo•soo
milk shake	**milk shake** *milk shake*
mint	**mentol** men•toll
monkfish	**ikan kera** ee•kahn kə•rah
mushroom	**jamur** jah•moor
mussel	**remis/kepah** rə•miss/kə•pah
mustard	**mustard** *mustard*
mutton	**daging domba** dah•ging dom•bah
noodle	**mie** mee
nutmeg	**buah pala** boo•wah pah•lah
nuts	**kacang** kah•chahng
octopus	**gurita** goo•ree•tah
okra [lady's finger]	**okra** *okra*
olive	**zaitun** zye•toon

olive oil	**minyak zaitun** *mee·nyahk zye·toon*
omelet	**telur dadar** *tə·loor dahn·dahr*
onion	**bawang** *bah·wahng*
orange	**jeruk** *jə·rook*
oregano	**oregano** *oregano*
organ meat [offal]	**jerohan** *jə·ro·wahn*
ox	**sapi jantan** *sah·pee jahn·tahn*
oxtail	**buntut sapi** *boon·toot sah·pee*
oyster	**tiram** *tee·rahm*
palm sugar	**gula palem** *goo·lah pah·ləm*
pancake	**panekuk** *pah·nə·kook*
papaya	**pepaya** *pə·pah·yah*
paprika	**paprika** *pah·pree·kah*
pastry	**pastry** *pastry*
peach	**peach** *peach*
peanut [groundnut]	**kacang** *kah·chahng*
pear	**pir** *pir*
peas	**ercis** *er·chis*
pecan	**pecan** *pecan*
pepper (black/white)	**lada (hitam/putih)** *lahn·dah (hee·tahm/poo·teeh)*
pepper [chilli]	**cabai** *chah·bye*

pheasant	**burung kuau** *boo·roong koo·wow*
pickle	**acar** *ah·chahr*
pie	**pai** *pie*
pineapple	**nanas** *nah·nahs*
pizza	**pizza** *pizza*
plum	**plum** *plum*
pomegranate	**delima** *də·lee·mah*
pork	**babi** *bah·bee*
port	**port** *port*
potato	**kentang** *kən·tahng*
potato chips [crisps]	**keripik kentang** *kə·ree·pick kən·tahng*
poultry	**unggas** *oong·gahs*
prune	**prun** *proon*
pumpkin	**labu merah** *lah·boo meh·rah*
quail	**burung puyuh** *boo·roong poo·yooh*
rabbit	**kelinci** *kə·lin·chee*
radish	**lobak** *loh·bhak*
raisin	**kismis** *kiss·miss*
red cabbage	**kol merah** *kol meh·rah*
relish	**penyedap rasa** *pə·nyə·dahp rah·sah*
rice	**beras** *bə·rahs*

roast	**panggang** *pahng·gahng*
roast beef	**sapi panggang** *sah·pee pahng·gahng*
rum	**rum** *room*
salad	**selada** *sə·lahn·dah*
salami	**salami** *salami*
salmon	**salmon** *sahl·mon*
salt	**garam** *gah·rahm*
sardine	**sarden** *sahr·den*
sauce	**saos** *sah·woss*
sausage	**sosis** *soh·sees*
scallion [spring onion]	**daun bawang** *dah·woon bah·wahng*
scallop	**kerang** *kə·rahng*
scotch	**scotch** *scotch*
sea bass	**bas laut** *bahs lah·woot*
sea perch	**ikan air tawar** *ee·kahn ah·yeer tah·wahr*
seafood	**seafood** *seafood*
seaweed	**rumput laut** *room·put lah·woot*
shallot	**bawang merah kecil** *bah·wahng meh·rah kə·cheel*
shank	**sekengkel** *sə·keng·kell*
shellfish	**kerang** *kə·rahng*
sherry	**sherry** *sherry*
shoulder	**bahu** *bah·hoo*
shrimp	**udang** *oo·dahng*
silver carp	**kerapu perak** *kə·rah·poo pe·rahk*
sirloin	**sirloin** *sirloin*
snack	**cemilan** *cə·mee·lahn*
snail	**siput** *see·poot*
soda	**soda** *soda*
soup	**sup** *soop*
sour cream	**krim asam** *krim ah·sahm*
soy [soya]	**kecap asin** *kə·chahp ah·sin*

soy sauce	**kecap**	kə·chahp
soybean [soya bean]	**kedelai**	kə·də·lye
soymilk [soya milk]	**susu kedelai**	soo·soo kə·də·lye
spaghetti	**spaghetti**	spaghetti
spices	**rempah**	rəm·pah
spinach	**bayam**	bah·yahm
spirits	**spirit**	spirit
squash	**labu siam**	lah·boo see·yahm
squid	**cumi**	choo·mee
steak	**steak**	steak
strawberry	**stroberi**	stroh·beh·ree
sugar	**gula**	goo·lah
sweets	**permen**	per·man
sweet and sour sauce	**saos asam manis**	sah·woss ah·sahm mah·niss
sweet corn	**jagung manis**	jah·goong mah·niss
sweet pepper	**lada manis**	lahn·dah mah·niss
sweet potato	**ubi**	oo·bee
sweetener	**pemanis**	pə·mah·niss
swordfish	**ikan cucut**	ee·kahn choo·choot
syrup	**sirop**	see·rop
tamarind	**asam**	ah·sahm
tangerine	**jeruk limau**	jə·rook lee·mow
tea	**teh**	teh
tofu	**tahu**	tah·hoo
toast	**toast**	toast
tomato	**tomat**	toh·maht
tongue	**lidah**	lee·dah
tonic water	**air tonic**	ah·yeer tonic
tripe	**babat**	bah·baht
trout	**trout**	trout
tuna	**tuna**	tuna

turkey	**ayam kalkun** *ah•yahm kahl•koon*
turnip	**lobak china** *loh•bahk chee•nah*
vanilla	**vanilla** *vanilla*
veal	**anak sapi** *ah•nahk sah•pee*
vegetable	**sayuran** *sah•yoo•rahn*
venison	**daging rusa** *dah•ging roo•sah*
vinegar	**cuka** *choo•kah*
vodka	**vodka** *vodka*
waffle	**wafel** *wah•fəl*
walnut	**kenari** *kə•nah•ree*
watercress	**seledri air** *sə•le•dree ah•yeer*
watermelon	**semangka** *sə•mahng•kah*
wheat	**gandum** *gahn•doom*
whisky	**whisky** *whisky*
wine	**wine** *wine*
yogurt	**yogurt** *yogurt*
zucchini	**zucchini** *zucchini*

Indonesian cuisine is hard to define. Thousands of islands make up the Indonesian archipelago, and each island boasts its own local culture, customs, and culinary specialties. In general, Indonesian cooking is rice-based. Well-known Indonesian dishes include: **nasi goreng** (fried rice with various savory toppings), **nasi padang** (steamed rice served with curry and a smorgasbord of local delicacies), **soto** (a soup, of which there are many different local versions), and **sate** (sweet and savory barbecued meat).

Some Indonesian dishes may be extremely spicy, with chillies added liberally to the food or accompanying sauce. If you are unsure, you can ask if the dish is spicy (**pedas**) and request for it to be made less so (**jangan pedas-pedas**).

People

ESSENTIAL

Hello!	**Halo!** *hah·loh*
How are you?	**Apa kabar?** *ah·pah kah·bar*
Fine, thanks.	**Baik, terima kasih.** *bah·yeek, tə·ree·mah kah·seeh*
Excuse me!	**Maaf!** *mah·ahf*
Do you speak English?	**Apakah anda bisa berbicara dalam bahasa Inggris?** *ah·pah·kah ahn·dah bee·sah bər·bee·chah·rah dah·lahm bah·hah·sah ing·grees*
What's your name?	**Siapa nama anda?** *see·yah·pah nah·mah ahn·dah*
My name is...	**Nama saya...** *nah·mah sah·yah*
Nice to know you.	**Senang berkenalan dengan anda.** *sə·nahng bər·kə·nah·lahn də·ngahn ahn·dah*
Where are you from?	**Anda dari mana?** *ahn·dah dah·ree mah·nah*
I'm from the U.S./U.K.	**Saya dari Amerika/Inggris.** *sah·yah dah·ree ah·meh·ree·kah/ing·grees*
What do you do?	**Apa pekerjaan anda?** *ah·pah pə·kər·jah·ahn ahn·dah*
I work as...	**Saya bekerja sebagai...** *sah·yah bə·kər·jah sə·bah·gye*
I work for...	**Saya bekerja untuk...** *sah·yah bə·kər·jah oon·took*
I'm a student.	**Saya seorang pelajar.** *sah·yah sə·oh·rahng pə·lah·jar*
I'm retired.	**Saya sudah pensiun.** *sah·yah soo·dah pen·see·yoon*
Do you like...?	**Apakah anda suka...?** *ah·pah·kah ahn·dah soo·kah*
Goodbye.	**Selamat tinggal.** *sə·lah·maht ting·gahl*

It is polite to address people using:

Bapak/Mas *bah·pahk/mahs*   Mr

Ibu *ee·boo*   Madam/Mrs

Mbak *mbahk*   Miss/Ms

You may also come across titles like '**Raden**', '**Rangkayo**', and '**Yang Terhormat**'. These are titles awarded by the nation to individuals who have made noteworthy contributions. They are usually people who hold high positions in society, and politicians.

Language Difficulties

| Do you speak English? | **Apakah anda bisa berbicara dalam bahasa Inggris?** *ah·pah·kah ahn·dah bee·sah bar·bee·chah·rah dah·lahm bah·hah·sah ing·grees* |
| Does anyone here speak English? | **Apakah di sini ada yang bisa berbicara dalam bahasa Inggris?** *ah·pah·kah dee·see·nee ah·dah yahng bee·sah bar·bee·chah·rah dah·lahm bah·hah·sah ing·grees* |

I don't speak Indonesian.	**Saya tidak bisa bicara bahasa Indonesia.** *sah•yah tee•dahk bee•sah bee•chah•rah bah•hah•sah in•doh•neh•shah*
Can you speak more slowly?	**Bisakah anda bicara lebih pelan?** *bee•sah•kah ahn•dah bee•chah•rah lə•beeh pə•lahn*
Can you repeat that?	**Bisa diulangi?** *bee•sah dee•oo•lah•ngee*
Excuse me?	**Maaf?** *mah•ahf*
What was that?	**Apa itu?** *ah•pah ee•too*
Can you spell it?	**Bisa anda eja?** *bee•sah ahn•dah eh•jah*
Please write it down.	**Tolong tuliskan.** *toh•long too•liss•kahn*
Can you translate this into English for me?	**Bisakah anda menerjemahkan ini ke bahasa Inggris untuk saya?** *bee•sah•kah ahn•dah mə•nər•jə•mah•kahn ee•nee kə bah•hah•sah ing•grees oon•took sah•yah*
What does this/that mean?	**Apa artinya ini/itu?** *ah•pah ahr•tee•nyah ee•nee/ee•too*
I understand.	**Saya mengerti.** *sah•yah mə•ngər•tee*
I don't understand.	**Saya tidak mengerti.** *sah•yah tee•dahk mə•ngər•tee*
Do you understand?	**Anda mengerti?** *ahn•dah mə•ngər•tee*

YOU MAY HEAR...

Saya hanya bisa bicara bahasa Inggris sedikit. *sah•yah hah•nyah bee•sah bee•chah• rah bah•hah•sah ing•grees sə•dee•kit*	I only speak a little English.
Saya tidak bisa bicara bahasa Inggris. *sah•yah tee•dahk bee•sah bee•chah•rah bah•hah•sah ing•grees*	I don't speak English.

Indonesians smile a lot, and are generally polite, helpful, hospitable and friendly. Say hello and they will immediately return your greeting and possibly strike up a conversation.

Making Friends

Hello!	**Halo!** *hah·loh*
Good morning.	**Selamat pagi.** *sə·lah·maht pah·gee*
Good afternoon.	**Selamat siang.** *sə·lah·maht see·yahng*
Good evening.	**Selamat malam.** *sə·lah·maht mah·lahm*
My name is...	**Nama saya...** *nah·mah sah·yah*
What's your name?	**Siapa nama anda?** *see·yah·pah nah·mah ahn·dah*
I'd like to introduce you to...	**Saya ingin perkenalkan anda kepada...** *sah·yah ee·ngin pər·kə·nahl·kahn ahn·dah kə·pah·dah*
Pleased to meet you.	**Senang bertemu anda.** *sə·nahng bər·tə·moo ahn·dah*
How are you?	**Apa kabar?** *ah·pah kah·bar*
Fine, thank you.	**Kabar baik, terima kasih.** *kah·bar bah·yeek, tə·ree·mah kah·seeh*

Travel Talk

I'm here...	**Saya di sini...** *sah·yah dee see·nee*
on business	**untuk urusan bisnis** *oon·took oo·roo·sahn biss·niss*
on vacation [holiday]	**berlibur** *bər·lee·boor*
studying	**belajar** *bə·lah·jar*
I'm staying for...	**Saya tinggal selama...** *sah·yah ting·gahl sə·lah·mah*

I've been here…	**Saya sudah berada di sini…** *sah•yah soo•dah bər•ah•dah dee see•nee*
a day	**sehari** *sə•hah•ree*
a week	**seminggu** *sə•ming•goo*
a month	**sebulan** *sə•boo•lahn*
Where are you from?	**Anda dari mana?** *ahn•dah dah•ree mah•nah*
I'm from…	**Saya dari…** *sah•yah dah•ree*
Have you ever been to…?	**Apakah anda pernah ke…?** *ah•pah•kah ahn•dah pər•nah kə*
Australia	**Australia** *os•trah•lee•yah*
Canada	**Kanada** *kah•nah•dah*
Ireland	**Irlandia** *ir•lahn•dee•yah*
the U.K.	**Inggris** *ing•grees*
the U.S.	**Amerika** *ah•meh•ree•kah*

For Numbers, see page 169.

Personal

Who are you with?	**Anda dengan siapa?** *ahn·dah də·ngahn see·yah·pah*
I'm here alone.	**Saya di sini sendirian.** *sah·yah dee see·nee sən·dee·ree·yahn*
I'm with my...	**Saya bersama...** *sah·yah bər·sah·mah*
husband/wife	**suami/istri** *soo·wah·mee/is·tree*
boyfriend/ girlfriend	**pacar** *pah·chahr*
friend(s)	**teman** *tə·mahn*
colleague(s)	**kolega** *koh·leh·gah*
When's your birthday?	**Kapan ulang tahun anda?** *kah·pahn oo·lahng tah·hoon ahn·dah*
How old are you?	**Berapa usia anda?** *bə·rah·pah oo·see·yah ahn·dah*
I'm...	**Saya...** *sah·yah*
Are you married?	**Apakah anda sudah menikah?** *ah·pah·kah ahn·dah soo·dah mə·nee·kah*
I'm...	**Saya...** *sah·yah*
single/in a relationship	**lajang/sudah punya pacar** *lah·jahng/soo·dah poo·nyah pah·chahr*
engaged/married	**bertunangan/menikah** *bər·too·nah·ngahn/ mə·nee·kah*
divorced/separated	**sudah bercerai/berpisah** *oo·dah bər·chə·rye/ bər·pee·sah*
a widower	**duda** *doo·dah*
a widow	**janda** *jahn·dah*
Do you have children/ grandchildren?	**Anda punya anak/cucu?** *ahn·dah poo·nyah ah·nahk/choo·choo*

For Numbers, see page 169.

Work & School

What do you do?	**Apa pekerjaan anda?** *ah·pah pa·kar·jah·ahn ahn·dah*
What are you studying?	**Anda belajar apa?** *ahn·dah ba·lah·jar ah·pah*
I'm learning Indonesian.	**Saya belajar bahasa Indonesia.** *sah·yah ba·lah·jar bah·hah·sah in·doh·neh·shah*
I...	**Saya...** *sah·yah*
am a consultant	**konsultan** *kon·sool·than*
work full-time/ part-time	**bekerja purna waktu/paruh waktu** *ba·kar·jah poor·nah wahk·too/pah·rooh wahk·too*
am unemployed	**nganggur** *ngahng·goor*
work at home	**bekerja di rumah** *ba·kar·jah dee roo·mah*
Who do you work for?	**Anda bekerja untuk siapa?** *ahn·dah ba·kar·jah oon·took see·yah·pah*
I work for...	**Saya bekerja untuk...** *sah·yah ba·kar·jah oon·took*
Here's my business card.	**Ini kartu nama saya.** *ee·nee kar·too nah·mah sah·yah*

For Business Travel, see page 142.

Weather

What's the forecast?	**Bagaimana ramalan cuaca?** *bah·gye·mah·nah rah·mah·lahn choo·wah·chah*
What beautiful/ terrible weather!	**Betapa indah/buruk cuacanya!** *ba·tah·pah in·dah/boo·rook choo·wah·chah·nyah*
It's...	**Cuacanya...** *choo·wah·chah·nyah*
cool/warm	**sejuk/hangat** *sa·jook/hah·ngaht*
cold/hot	**dingin/panas** *dee·ngin/pah·nahs*
rainy/sunny	**hujan/cerah** *hoo·jahn/cha·rah*
Do I need a jacket/ an umbrella?	**Apakah saya perlu jaket/payung?** *ah·pah·kah sah·yah par·loo jah·ket/pah·yoong*

For Temperature, see page 175.

Romance

ESSENTIAL

Would you like to go out for a drink/dinner?	**Anda mau pergi minum/makan malam?** *ahn·dah mah·woo pər·gee mee·noom/ mah·kahn mah·lahm*
What are your plans for tonight/tomorrow?	**Apa rencana anda untuk malam ini/besok?** *ah·pah rən·chah·nah ahn·dah oon·took mah·lahm ee·nee/beh·sok*
Can I have your number?	**Bisa saya minta nomor telepon anda?** *bee·sah sah·yah min·tah noh·mor tə·lə·pon ahn·dah*
Can I join you?	**Bisa saya ikut dengan anda?** *bee·sah sah·yah ee·koot də·ngahn ahn·dah*
Can I get [treat] you a drink?	**Bisa saya belikan/traktir minum?** *bee·sah sah·yah bəh·lee·kahn/trakh·teer mee·noom*
I like/love you.	**Saya suka/cinta kepadamu.** *sah·yah soo·kah/ chin·tah kə·pah·dah·moo*

The Dating Game

Would you like to go out for coffee?	**Anda mau pergi keluar untuk minum kopi?** *ahn·dah mah·woo pər·gee kə·loo·wahr oon·took mee·noom koh·pee*
Would you like to go out for a drink/dinner?	**Maukah Anda pergi makan/minum bersama?** *mah·oo·kah Ahn·dah pər·gee mah·kahn/mee·noom bər·sah·mah*
What are your plans for...?	**Apa rencana anda untuk...?** *ah·pah rən·chah·nah ahn·dah oon·took*
today	**hari ini** *hah·ree ee·nee*
tonight	**malam ini** *mah·lahm ee·nee*

tomorrow	**besok** *beh·sok*
this weekend	**akhir pekan ini** *akh·khir pə·kan ee·nee*
Where would you like to go?	**Anda ingin pergi ke mana?** *ahn·dah ee·ngin pər·gee kə mah·nah*
I'd like to go to...	**Saya ingin pergi ke...** *sah·yah ee·ngin pər·gee kə*
Do you like...?	**Apakah anda suka...?** *ah·pah·kah ahn·dah soo·kah*
Can I have your number/e-mail?	**Bisa saya minta nomor telepon/ e-mail anda?** *bee·sah sah·yah min·tah noh·mor tə·lə·pon/e·mail ahn·dah*
Are you on Facebook/ Twitter?	**Anda ada di Facebook/Twitter?** *ahn·dah ah·dah di fehs·book/tweet·tər*
Can I join you?	**Bisa saya ikut dengan anda?** *bee·sah sah·yah ee·koot də·ngahn ahn·dah*
You're very attractive.	**Anda sangat menarik.** *ahn·dah sah·ngaht mə·nah·rik*
Let's go somewhere quieter.	**Mari kita pergi ke tempat yang lebih tenang.** *mah·ree kee·tah pər·gee kə təm·paht yahng lə·beeh tə·nahng*

For Communications, see page 52.

Accepting & Rejecting

I'd love to.	**Ya, saya mau.** *yah, sah·yah mah·woo.*
Where should we meet?	**Di mana kita ketemu?** *dee·mah·nah kee·tah kə·tə·moo*
I'll meet you at the bar/at your hotel.	**Saya temui anda di bar/di hotel anda.** *sah·yah tə·moo·wee ahn·dah dee bar/dee hoh·tell ahn·dah*
I'll come by at...	**Saya datang jam...** *sah·yah dah·tahng jahm*
What is your address?	**Alamat anda di mana?** *ah·lah·maht ahn·dah dee mah·nah*
I'm busy.	**Saya sibuk.** *sah·yah see·book*
I'm not interested.	**Saya tidak tertarik.** *sah·yah tee·dahk tər·tah·rik*

| Leave me alone. | **Tinggalkan saya.** *ting·gahl·kahn sah·yah* |
| Stop bothering me! | **Berhenti mengganggu saya!** *bər·hən·tee məng·gahng·goo sah·yah* |

Getting Intimate

Can I hug/kiss you?	**Bisa saya memeluk/mencium anda?** *bee·sah sah·yah mə·mə·look/mən·chee·yoom ahn·dah*
Yes.	**Ya.** *yah*
No.	**Tidak.** *tee·dahk*
I like/love you.	**Saya suka/cinta kepadamu.** *sah·yah soo·kah/ chin·tah kə·pah·dahmu*
Stop!	**Stop!** *stop*

Sexual Preferences

Are you gay?	**Apakah Anda penyuka sesama jenis?** *ah·pah·kah ahn·dah pə·nyoo·kah sə·sah·mah jə·nees*
I'm…	**Saya…** *Sah·yah*
heterosexual	**heteroseksual** *heh·tə·roh·sehk·soo·ahl*
homosexual	**homoseksual** *hoh·moh·sehk·soo·ahl*
bisexual	**biseksual** *bee·sehk·soo·ahl*
Do you like men/women ?	**Anda suka pria/wanita?** *ahn·dah soo·kah pree·ah/ wah·nee·tah*

Indonesians are generally reserved and may not be comfortable when asked forward or aggressive questions regarding romance or sexuality.

Leisure Time

Sightseeing

ESSENTIAL

Where's the tourist information office?	**Kantor informasi turis di mana?** *kahn•tor in•for•mah•see too•riss dee•mah•nah*
What are the main attractions (here)?	**Apa tempat utama yang menarik di sini?** *ah•pah təm•paht oo•tah•mah yahng mə•nah•rik dee see•nee*
Are there tours in English?	**Apakah ada tur yang berbahasa Inggris?** *ah•pah•kah ah•dah toor yahng bər•bah•hah•sah ing•grees*
Can I have a map?	**Bisa saya minta peta?** *bee•sah sah•yah min•tah pə•tah*
Can I have a guide book?	**Bisa saya minta buku panduan?** *bee•sah sah•yah min•tah boo•koo pahn•doo•wahn*

Tourist Information

Do you have information on...?	**Anda punya informasi tentang...?** *ahn•dah poo•nyah in•for•mah•see tən•tahng*
Can you recommend...?	**Dapatkah anda menyarankan...?** *dah•paht•kah ahn•dah mə•nyah•rahn•kahn*
a bus tour	**tur dengan bis** *toor də•ngahn bis*
an excursion to...	**darmawisata ke...** *dahr•mah•wee•sah•tah kə*
a sightseeing tour	**tur pemandangan** *toor pə•mahn•dah•ngahn*

On Tour

I'd like to go on the tour to...	**Saya ingin tur ke...** *sah•yah ee•ngin toor kə*
When's the next tour?	**Kapan tur berikutnya?** *kah•pahn toor bə•ree•koot•nyah*

Plenty of websites offer general and detailed information about visiting Indonesia. Here are some useful sites to try:

www.indonesia.travel

www.indonesiatourism.com

www.indonesia-tourism.com

Are there tours in English?	**Apakah ada tur yang berbahasa Inggris?** *ah•pah•kah ah•dah toor yahng bər•bah•hah•sah ing•grees*
Is there an English guide book?	**Apakah ada buku panduan dalam bahasa Inggris?** *ah•pah•kah ah•dah boo•koo pahn•doo•wahn dah•lahm bah•hah•sah ing•grees*
Is there an English audio guide?	**Apakah ada panduan audio (suara) dalam bahasa Inggris?** *ah•pah•kah ah•dah pahn•doo•wahn ow•dee•yoh (soo•wah•rah) dah•lahm bah•hah•sah Ing•grees*
What time do we leave/return?	**Kapan kita berangkat/kembali?** *kah•pahn kee•tah bə•rahng•kaht/kəm•bah•lee*
We'd like to see...	**Kami ingin melihat...** *kah•mee ee•ngin mə•lee•haht*

Can we stop here…?	**Dapatkah kita berhenti di sini…?** *dah•paht•kah kee•tah bər•hən•tee dee see•nee*
to take photos	**untuk berfoto** *oon•took bər•foh•toh*
for souvenirs	**untuk membeli suvenir** *oon•took məm•bə•lee soo•və•neer*
for the toilets	**untuk ke kamar kecil** *oon•took kə kah•mar kə•cheel*
Is it handicapped [disabled]- accessible?	**Apakah bisa dilalui oleh penyandang cacat?** *ah•pah•kah bee•sah dee•lah•loo•wee oh•leh pə•nyahn•dahng chah•chaht*

For Tickets, see page 20.

Seeing the Sights

Where is/are the…?	**…di mana?** *dee•mah•nah*
battleground	**medan pertempuran** *meh•dahn pər•təm•poor•ahn*
botanical garden	**kebun raya** *kə•boon rah•yah*
castle	**kastel** *kahs•teel*
city hall	**balai kota** *bah•lye koh•tah*
downtown area	**pusat kota** *poo•saht koh•tah*
fort	**benteng** *ben•teng*
fountain	**air mancur** *ah•yeer mahn•choor*
library	**perpustakaan** *pər•poos•tah•kah•ahn*
market	**pasar** *pah•sahr*
(war) memorial	**tugu peringatan (perang)** *too•goo pə•ree•ngah•tahn (pə•rahng)*
mosque	**mesjid** *məs•jid*
museum	**museum** *moo•seh•yoom*
nature reserve	**cagar alam** *chah•gar ah•lahm*
old town	**kota tua** *ko•tah too•wah*
opera house	**gedung opera** *gə•doong o•pə•rah*
palace	**istana** *iss•tah•nah*
park	**taman** *tah•mahn*

shopping area	**pusat perbelanjaan** *poo·saht pər·bə·lahn·jah·ahn*
temple	**candi/kuil** *chahn·dee/koo·weel*
theme park/resort	**taman/resor bertema (taman mini)** *tah·mahn/ re·sor bər·te·mah (tah·mahn mee·nee)*
town square	**alun-alun** *ah·loon·ah·loon*
Can you show me on the map?	**Bisa anda tunjukkan pada peta?** *bee·sah ahn·dah toon·joo·kahn pah·dah pə·tah*
Is it handicapped [disabled]- accessible?	**Apakah bisa dilalui oleh penyandang cacat?** *ah·pah·kah bee·sah dee·lah·loo·wee oh·leh pə·nyahn·dahng chah·chaht*
It's...	**Itu/Ini...** *ee·too/ee·nee*
amazing	**mengagumkan** *mə·ngah·goom·kahn*
beautiful	**indah/cantik** *in·dah/chahn·tik*
boring	**membosankan** *məm·bo·sahn·kahn*
interesting	**menarik** *mə·nah·rik*
magnificent	**luar biasa** *loo·wahr bee·yah·sah*
romantic	**romantis** *ro·mahn·tiss*
strange	**aneh** *ah·neh*
stunning	**mencengangkan** *mən·chə·ngahng·kahn*
terrible	**buruk sekali** *boo·rook sə·kah·lee*
ugly	**jelek** *jə·lek*

The majority of Indonesians practice Islam, and Indonesia has
the highest Muslim population in the world. The other main
religions are Buddhism, Christianity and Hinduism.
You may be asked to remove your shoes before entering a mosque,
or a Buddhist or Hindu temple as shoes are considered to bear the
impurities of the 'outside' world. (This restriction may also apply to
private homes. If you are not sure, do not be afraid to ask your host.)
There are not many food taboos, but you should avoid ordering a pork
dish when dining with Muslims or beef when eating with Hindus.

| I like it. | **Saya suka.** *sah·yah soo·kah* |
| I don't like it. | **Saya tidak suka.** *sah·yah tee·dahk soo·kah* |

For Asking Directions, see page 37.

Religious Sites

Where's...?	**Di mana letak...?** *dee mah·nah lə·tahk*
the cathedral	**katedral** *kah·teh·drahl*
the Catholic/	**gereja Katolik/Protestan** *gə·reh·jah*
Protestant church	*Kah·toh·lik/Proh·tehs·tahn*
the mosque	**masjid** *mahs·jeed*
the shrine	**kuil** *koo·eel*
the synagogue	**sinagog** *see·nah·goh·geh*
the temple	**pura** *poo·rah*
What time is the	**Pukul berapa layanannya?** *poo·kool bə·rah·pah*
service?	*lah·yahn·ahn·nyah*

ESSENTIAL

Where's the market?	**Pasar di mana?** *pah•sahr dee•mah•nah*
Where's the mall [shopping centre]?	**Mal di mana?** *mal dee•mah•nah*
I'm just looking.	**Saya hanya lihat-lihat.** *sah•yah hah•nyah lee•haht•lee•haht*
Can you help me?	**Bisa bantu/tolong saya?** *bee•sah bahn•too/ toh•long sah•yah*
I'm being helped.	**Saya sedang dibantu.** *sah•yah sə•dahng dee•bahn•too*
How much?	**Berapa harganya?** *bə•rah•pah har•gah•nyah*
That one, please.	**Tolong yang itu.** *toh•long yahng ee•too*
That's all.	**Itu saja.** *ee•too sah•jah*
Where can I pay?	**Di mana saya membayar?** *dee mah•nah sah•yah mə m•bah•yar*
I'll pay in cash.	**Saya bayar kontan/tunai.** *sah•yah bah•yahr kon•tahn/too•nay*
I'll pay by credit card.	**Saya bayar pakai kartu kredit.** *sah•yah bah•yahr pah•kye kahr•too kre•dit*
A receipt, please.	**Tolong tanda terimanya.** *toh•long tahn•dah tə•ree•mah•nyah*

At the Shops

Where's the…?	**…di mana?** *dee•mah•nah*
24-hr convenience store	**toko kelontong yang buka 24-jam** *toh•koh kə•lon•tong yahng boo•kah 24•jahm*
antiques store	**toko barang antik** *toh•koh bah•rahng ahn•tik*
bakery	**toko roti-kue** *toh•koh ro•tee•koo•weh*
bank	**bank** *bahng*
bookstore	**toko buku** *toh•koh boo•koo*
camera store	**toko kamera** *toh•koh kah•me•rah*
clothing store	**toko pakaian** *toh•koh pah•kah•yahn*
delicatessen	**makanan bercita rasa tinggi** *mah•kahn•ahn bər•chee•tah rah•sah teeng•gi*
department store	**pusat pertokoan** *poo•saht pər•toh•koh•wahn*
food/hawker centre	**pusat makanan/kakilima** *poo•saht mah•kah•nahn/kah•kee•lee•mah*
gift shop	**toko suvenir/cenderamata** *toh•koh soo•və•neer/cən•də•rah•mah•tah*
health food store	**toko makanan kesehatan** *toh•koh mah•kah•nahn kə•seh•hah•tahn*
jeweler	**toko perhiasan** *toh•koh pər•hee•yah•sahn*

Big shopping malls are a common sight in the cities, like
the capital Jakarta. Elsewhere, small shops and roadside stalls
and vendors dominate. Traditional art and craft items, and quirky
souvenirs are the usual tourist favorites.

Most stall owners and vendors expect you to bargain over the price,
and goods are often offered at a higher price initially. The final amount
transacted is open to negotiation, so don't be afraid to haggle.
However, shopping centers have fixed prices, so bargaining does not
apply here.

liquor store	**toko minuman keras** *toh·koh*	
(off-licence)	*mee·noo· mahn kə·rahs*	
market	**pasar** *pah·sahr*	
music [CD] store	**toko musik** *toh·koh moo·sik*	
night market	**pasar malam** *pah·sahr mah·lahm*	
pastry shop	**toko kue** *toh·koh koo·weh*	
pharmacy	**apotek** *ah·po·tek*	
produce store	**toko bahan makanan**	
[grocery]	*toh·koh bah·hahn mah·kah·nahn*	
shoe store	**toko sepatu** *toh·koh sə·pah·too*	
shopping mall	**mal perbelanjaan** *mal pər·bə·lahn·jah·ahn*	
[shopping centre]		
souvenir store	**toko suvenir/cenderamata** *toh·koh soo·və·neer/*	
	cən·də·rah·mah·tah	
supermarket	**supermarket** *su·per·mar·ket*	
tobacconist	**pedagang tembakau**	
	pə·dah·gahng təm·bah·kow	
toy store	**toko mainan** *toh·koh mah·yee·nahn*	

YOU MAY SEE...

BUKA *boo·kah*	open
TUTUP *too·toop*	closed
TUTUP UNTUK MAKAN SIANG	closed for lunch
too·toop oon·took mah·kahn see·yahng	
RUANG PAS *roo·wahng pahs*	fitting room
KASIR *kah·seer*	cashier
BAYAR KONTAN *bah·yahr kon·tahn*	cash only
MENERIMA KARTU KREDIT	credit cards accepted
mə·nə·ree·mah kah·too kre·dit	
JAM BUKA *jahm boo·kah*	business hours
KELUAR *kə·loo·wahr*	exit

Ask an Assistant

When do you open/close?	**Kapan anda buka/tutup?** *kah·pahn ahn·dah boo·kah/too·toop*
Where's the...?	**...di mana?** *dee·mah·nah*
cashier	**kasir** *kah·seer*
escalator	**eskalator** *ess·kah·lah·tor*
elevator [lift]	**lift** *lift*
fitting room	**ruang pas** *roo·wahng pahs*
store directory	**direktori toko** *dee·rek·toh·ree toh·koh*
Can you help me?	**Bisa bantu/tolong saya?** *bee·sah bahn·too/toh·long sah·yah*
I'm just looking.	**Saya hanya lihat-lihat.** *sah·yah hah·nyah lee·haht·lee·haht*
I'm being helped.	**Saya sedang dibantu.** *sah·yah sə·dahng dee·bahn·too*
Do you have...?	**Anda punya...?** *ahn·dah poo·nyah*

YOU MAY HEAR...

Ada yang dapat saya bantu?   Can I help you?
ah•dah yahng dah•paht sah•yah bahn•too

Tunggu sebentar.   One moment. [Hold on.]
toong•goo sə•ben•tar

Anda ingin apa?   What would you like?
ahn•dah ee•ngin ah•pah

Ada lagi lainnya?   Anything else?
ah•dah lah•gee lah•yeen•nyah

Can you show me...?	**Bisa tolong tunjukkan...?** *bee•sah toh•long toon•joo•kahn*
Can you ship it?	**Bisa anda kirimkan?** *bee•sah ahn•dah kee•rim•kahn*
Can you wrap it?	**Bisa anda bungkus?** *bee•sah ahn•dah boong•koos*
How much?	**Berapa harganya?** *bə•rah•pah har•gah•nyah*
That's all.	**Itu saja.** *ee•too sah•jah*

For Clothing, see page 123.

For Souvenirs, see page 130.

In Indonesia, the most commonly accepted form of payment is cash. Major credit cards may be accepted at larger stores in city centers or popular tourist destinations.

Personal Preferences

I'd like something…	**Saya mau sesuatu yang…**	*sah•yah mah•woo sə•soo•wah•too yahng*
cheap/expensive	**murah/mahal**	*moo•rah/mah•hahl*
larger/smaller	**lebih besar/lebih kecil**	*lə•beeh bə•sahr/lə•beeh kə•cheel*
nicer	**lebih bagus**	*lə•beeh bah•goos*
from this region/ district	**dari wilayah/distrik ini**	*dah•ree wee•lah•yah/dis•trik ee•nee*
Around…Rupiah.	**Sekitar…Rupiah.**	*sə•kee•tahr…roo•pee•yah.*
Is it real?	**Ini asli?**	*ee•nee ahs•lee*
Can you show me this/that?	**Bisa anda tunjukkan ini/itu?**	*bee•sah ahn•dah toon•joo•kahn ee•nee/ee•too*
That's not quite what I want.	**Bukan itu yang saya mau.**	*boo•kahn ee•too yahng sah•yah mah•woo*
No, I don't like it.	**Tidak, saya tidak suka ini.**	*tee•dahk, sah•yah tee•dahk soo•kah ee•nee*
It's too expensive.	**Ini terlalu mahal.**	*ee•nee tər•lah•loo mah•hahl*
I have to think about it.	**Saya harus pikir-pikir dulu.**	*sah•yah hah•roos pee•keer•pee•keer doo•loo*
I'll take it.	**Saya ambil yang ini.**	*sah•yah ahm•beel yahng ee•nee*

Paying & Bargaining

How much?	**Berapa harganya?** *bə·rah·pah har·gah·nyah*
I'll pay. . .	**Saya akan bayar. . .** *sah·yah ah·kahn bah·yahr*
in cash	**kontan** *kon·tahn*
by credit card	**pakai kartu kredit** *pah·kye kar·too kre·dit*
by traveler's check [cheque]	**pakai cek wisata** *pah·kye check wee·sah·tah*
Can I use this. . .?	**Bisakah saya pakai. . .?** *bee·sah·kah sah·yah pah·kye*
ATM card	**kartu ATM** *kar·too ah·teh·em*
credit card	**kartu kredit** *kar·too kreh·dit*
debit card	**kartu debit** *kar·too deh·bit*
gift voucher	**kupon hadiah** *koo·pon hah·dee·yah*
How do I use this machine?	**Bagaimana cara menggunakan mesin ini?** *bah·gay·mah·nah chah·rah məng·goo·nah·kahn mə·sin ee·nee*
A receipt, please.	**Tolong tanda terimanya.** *toh·long tahn·dah tə·ree·mah·nyah*
That's too much.	**Itu kemahalan.** *ee·too kə·mah·hah·lahn*
I'll give you. . .	**Saya bayar anda. . .** *sah·yah bah·yahr ahn·dah*
I have only. . . Rupiah.	**Saya hanya punya. . . Rupiah** *sah·yah hah·nyah poo·nyah. . . roo·pee·yah*
Is that your best price?	**Apakah sudah harga pas?** *ah·pah·kah soo·dah har·gah pass*
Can you give me a discount?	**Bisa beri saya diskon?** *bee·sah bə·ree sah·yah dis·kon*

For Numbers, see page 169.

YOU MAY HEAR...

Bagaimana anda mau membayarnya?
bah·gye·mah·nah ahn·dah mah·woo mǝm·bah·yahr·nyah

How are you paying?

Kartu kredit anda ditolak.
kahr·too kreh·dit ahn·dah dee·to·lahk

Your credit card has been declined.

Tolong, tanda pengenal anda.
toh·long, tahn·dah pǝ·ngǝ·nahl Ahn·dah

ID, please.

Kami tidak menerima kartu kredit.
kah·mee tee·dahk mǝ·nǝ·ree·mah kahr·too kreh·dit

We don't accept credit cards.

Tolong bayar kontan saja.
toh·long bah·yahr kon·tahn sah·jah

Cash only, please.

Anda punya uang kecil?
ahn·dah poo·nyah oo·wahng kǝ·cheel

Do you have change/ small bills [notes]?

Making a Complaint

I'd like...	**Saya mau...** *sah·yah mah·woo*	
to exchange this	**menukar ini** *mǝ·noo·kar ee·nee*	
a refund	**minta uang saya kembali** *min·tah oo·wahng sah·yah kǝm·bah·lee*	
to see the manager	**bertemu manajer** *bǝr·tǝ·moo me·ne·jǝr*	

Services

Can you recommend...?	**Dapatkah anda menyarankan...?** *dah·paht·kah ahn·dah mǝ·nyah·rahn·kahn*
a barber	**tempat cukur rambut** *tǝm·paht choo·koor rahm·boot*
a dry cleaner	**dry clean (cuci kering)** *dry clean (choo·chee kǝ·ring)*
a hairstylist	**salon rambut** *sah·lon rahm·boot*

a laundromat [launderette]	**laundromat** *laundromat*
a nail salon	**salon pedikur/manikur** *sah•lon pe•dee•koor/ mah•nee•koor*
a spa	**spa** *spa*
a travel agency	**biro perjalanan** *bee•ro pər•jah•lah•nahn*
Can you...this?	**Bisa tolong...ini?** *bee•sah to•long...ee•nee*
alter	**ganti** *gahn•tee*
clean	**bersihkan** *bər•seeh•kahn*
fix [mend]	**perbaiki** *pər•bah•yee•kee*
press	**setrika** *sə•tree•kah*
When will it be ready?	**Kapan selesai?** *kah•pahn sə•lə•sye*

Hair & Beauty

I'd like...	**Saya mau...** *sah•yah mah•woo*
an appointment for today/ tomorrow	**buat janji untuk hari ini/besok** *boo•waht jahn•jee oon•took hah•ree ee•nee/ beh•sok*
some color/ highlights	**cat/ highlight rambut** *chaht/highlight rahm•boot*

my hair	**blow dry rambut**
blow-dried	*blow dry rahm·boot*
my hair styled	**menata rambut** *mə·nah·tah rahm·boot*
a haircut	**gunting rambut** *goon·ting rahm·boot*
a trim	**trim rambut** *trim rahm·boot*
Not too short.	**Jangan terlalu pendek.** *jah·ngahn tər·lah·loo pen·dek*
Shorter here.	**Di bagian ini lebih pendek.** *dee bah·gee·yahn ee·nee lə·beeh pen·dek*
I'd like…	**Saya mau…** *sah·yah mah·woo*
a facial	**facial** *facial*
a manicure	**manikur** *mah·nee·koor*
a pedicure	**pedikur** *pe·dee·koor*
an eyebrow wax	**cukur bikini** *choo·koor bee·kee·ni*
a bikini wax	**cukur alis** *choo·koor ah·lees*
a body massage	**pijat tubuh** *pee·jaht too·booh*
Do you have/do…?	**Apakah Anda ada/bisa…?** *ah·pah·kah ahn·dah ah·dah/bee·sah*
acupuncture	**akupunktur** *ah·koo·poong·toor*
aromatherapy	**aromaterapi** *ah·ro·mah·te·rah·pee*
oxygen treatment	**perawatan oksigen** *pə·rah·waht·ahn ohk·see·gehn*
a sauna	**sauna** *sah·woo·nah*

Antiques

How old is it?	**Setua apa ini?** *sə·too·wah ah·pah ee·nee*
Do you have anything from the…period?	**Apakah anda punya sesuatu dari masa…?** *ah·pah·kah ahn·dah poo·nyah sə·soo·wah·too dah·ree mah·sah*
Do I have to fill out any forms?	**Apakah saya harus mengisi formulir?** *ah·pah·kah sah·yah hah·roos mə·ngee·see for·moo·leer*

| Is there a certificate of authenticity? | **Apakah ada sertifikat keaslian?** *ah·pah·kah ah·dah sər·tee·fee·kaht kə·ahs·lee·yahn* |
| Can you ship/wrap it? | **Bisakah Anda mengirim/membungkusnya?** *bee·sah·kah ahn·dah mə·ngee·reem/ məm·boong·koos·nyah* |

Clothing

I'd like...	**Saya mau...** *sah·yah mah·woo*
Can I try this on?	**Bisa saya coba ini?** *bee·sah sah·yah cho·bah ee·nee*
It doesn't fit.	**Ini tidak pas.** *ee·nee tee·dahk pahs*
It's too...	**Ini terlalu...** *ee·nee tər·lah·loo*
big/small	**besar/kecil** *bə·sahr/kə·cheel*
short/long	**pendek/panjang** *pen·dek/pahn·jahng*
tight/loose	**sempit/longgar** *səm·pit/long·gar*
Do you have this in size...?	**Apa anda punya yang ukurannya...?** *ah·pah ahn·dah poo·nyah yahng oo·koo·rahn·nyah*
Do you have this in a bigger/smaller size?	**Apa anda punya ini yang ukurannya lebih besar/lebih kecil?** *ah·pah ahn·dah poo·nyah ee·nee yahng oo·koo·rahn·nyah lə·beeh bə·sahr/ la·beeh kə·cheel*

For Numbers, see page 169.

YOU MAY HEAR...

Anda bagus pakai itu.
ahn•dah bah•goos pah•kye ee•too

That looks great on you.

Apakah pas? *ah•pah•kah pahs*

How does it fit?

Kami tidak punya ukuran anda. *kah•mee tee•dahk poo•nyah oo•koo•rahn ahn•dah*

We don't have your size.

The making of **batik** cloth is a form of art in Indonesia. **Batik** painting, music and dance were considered higher art forms in the ancient Javanese courts. Today, **batik** is commonly worn as sarongs and used for the traditional women's dress known as '**kebaya**'. In Bali, **songket** cloth (a brocade with metallic thread) and **ikat** cloth produced by the local weavers make a unique and exquisite souvenir.

Colors

I'd like something…	**Saya mau sesuatu yang…** *sah·yah mah·woo sə·soo·wah·too yahng*
beige	**gading tua** *gah·ding too·wah*
black	**hitam** *hee·tahm*
blue	**biru** *bee·roo*
brown	**cokelat** *cho·kə·laht*
green	**hijau** *hee·jow*
gray	**abu-abu** *ah·boo·ah·boo*
orange	**oranye** *oh·rah·nyə*
pink	**merah muda** *meh·rah moo·dah*
purple	**ungu** *oo·ngoo*
red	**merah** *meh·rah*
white	**putih** *poo·teeh*
yellow	**kuning** *koo·ning*

Clothes & Accessories

backpack	**ransel** *rahn·səl*
batik shirt	**kemeja batik** *kə·me·jah batik*
belt	**ikat pinggang** *ee·kaht ping·gahng*
bikini	**bikini** *bee·kee·nee*
blouse	**blus** *bloos*
bra	**BH** *beh·hah*
briefs [underpants]	**celana dalam** *chə·lah·nah dah·lahm*

panties	**celana dalam wanita** che·lah·nah dah·lahm wah·nee·tah
coat	**jas** jahs
dress	**baju** bah·joo
hat	**topi** toh·pee
jacket	**jaket** jah·ket
jeans	**jeans** jeans
pajamas	**piyama** pee·yah·mah
pants [trousers]	**celana panjang** chə·lah·nah pahn·jahng
pantyhose [tights]	**pantyhose** pantyhose
handbag	**tas tangan** tahs tah·ngahn
purse	**tas kecil** tahs kə·cheel
raincoat	**jas hujan** jahs hoo·jahn
scarf	**syal** shahl
shirt	**kemeja** kə·meh·jah
shorts	**celana pendek** chə·lah·nah pen·dek
skirt	**rok** rok
socks	**kaos kaki** kah·woss kah·kee
suit	**jas** jahs
sunglasses	**kacamata hitam** kah·chah·mah·tah hee·tahm
sweater	**sweater** sweater
sweatshirt	**kaos** kah·woss
swimsuit	**pakaian renang** pah·kah·yahn rə·nahng
T-shirt	**kaos oblong** kah·woss oh·blong
tie	**dasi** dah·see
underwear	**pakaian dalam** pah·kah·yahn dah·lahm
wallet	**dompet** dom·pet

Fabric

I'd like...	**Saya mau...** sah·yah mah·woo
batik	**batik** batik
cotton	**katun** kah·toon

denim	**denim** *denim*
lace	**renda** *ren·dah*
leather	**kulit** *koo·leet*
linen	**linen** *lee·nen*
silk	**sutera** *soo·trah*
silk brocade	**brokat sutera** *bro·kaht soo·trah*
wool	**wol** *wol*
Is it machine washable?	**Ini bisa dicuci dengan mesin cuci?** *ee·nee bee·sah dee·choo·chee da·ngahn ma·sin choo·chee*

Shoes

I'd like...	**Saya mau...** *sah·yah mah·woo*
high-heels/flats	**sepatu tinggi/flat** *sa·pah·too ting·gee/flat*
boots	**sepatu bot** *sa·pah·too bot*
loafers	**sendal** *san·dahl*
sandals	**sendal** *san·dahl*
shoes	**sepatu** *sa·pah·too*
slippers	**selop** *sa·lop*
sneakers	**sepatu kanvas** *sa·pah·too kahn·vahs*
In size...	**Ukuran...** *oo·koo·rahn*

For Numbers, see page 169.

Sizes

chest measurement	**ukuran dada** *oo·koo·rahn dah·dah*
waist measurement	**ukuran pinggang** *oo·koo·rahn ping·gahng*
height	**tinggi** *ting·gee*
extra small (XS)	**ekstra kecil (XS)** *eks·trah kə·cheel (XS)*
small (S)	**kecil (S)** *kə·cheel (S)*
medium (M)	**medium (M)** *meh·dee·yoom (M)*
large (L)	**besar (L)** *bə·sahr (L)*
extra large (XL)	**ekstra besar (XL)** *eks·trah bə·sahr (XL)*
petite	**kecil** *kə·cheel*
plus size	**ukuran plus** *oo·koo·rahn ploos*

Newsagent & Tobacconist

Do you sell English-language newspapers?	**Ada koran bahasa Inggris?** *ah·dah ko·rahn bah·hah·sah ing·grees*
I'd like...	**Saya mau...** *sah·yah mah·woo*
candy [sweets]	**permen [manisan]** *pər·mehn [mah·nees·ahn]*
chewing gum	**permen karet** *pər·mehn kah·reht*
a cigar	**cerutu** *chə·roo·too*

There are numerous newspapers available in Indonesian, English and Chinese. Most have online editions too.

a pack/carton of cigarettes	**satu pak/boks rokok** *sah·too pahk/boks roh·kok*
I'd like...	**Saya mau...** *sah·yah mah·woo*
a lighter	**pemantik api** *pə·mahn·tik ah·pee*
a magazine	**majalah** *mah·jah·lah*
matches	**korek api** *koh·rek ah·pee*
a newspaper	**koran/surat kabar** *ko·rahn/soo·raht kah·bar*
a pen	**pena** *pə·nah*
a phone card	**kartu telepon** *kar·too tə·lə·pon*
a postcard	**kartu pos** *kar·too pos*
a road/town map of...	**peta jalan/kota...** *pə·tah jah·lahn/koh·tah*
stamps	**perangko** *pə·rahng·koh*

Photography

I'd like a/an... camera.	**Saya ingin kamera...** *sah·yah ee·ngin kah·meh·rah*
automatic	**otomatis** *oh·toh·mah·tees*
digital	**digital** *dee·gee·tahl*
disposable	**sekali pakai** *sə·kah·lee pah·kye*
I'd like...	**Saya mau...** *sah·yah mah·woo*
a battery	**baterai** *bah·tə·rye*
digital prints	**cetak foto digital** *cheh·tahk foh·toh dee·gee·tahl*
a memory card	**kartu memori** *khr·too meh·mo·ree*
Can I print digital photos here?	**Bisa cetak foto digital di sini?** *bee·sah cheh·tahk fo·to dee·gee·tahl dee see·nee*

Souvenirs

book	**buku**	boo·koo
box of chocolates	**sekotak cokelat**	sə·ko·tahk cho·kə·laht
painting	**lukisan**	loo·kee·sahn
batik cloth	**kain batik**	kah·yeen batik
batik clothes	**pakaian batik**	pah·kah·yahn batik
costume jewelry	**perhiasan murah**	pər·hee·yah·sahn moo·rahh
doll	**boneka**	boh·neh·kah
key ring [chain]	**gantungan kunci**	gahn·too·ngahn koon·chee
lacquerware	**barang yang dipernis**	bah·rahng yahng dee·per·niss
pewter-ware	**barang dari alpaka**	bah·rahng dah·ree ahl·pah·kah
porcelain	**porselen**	por·sə·len
postcard	**kartu pos**	kar·too pos
pottery	**barang tembikar**	bah·rahng təm·bee·kar
rattan basket	**keranjang rotan**	kə·rahn·jahng roh·tahn
silk	**sutera**	soo·trah
silk brocade	**brokat sutera**	broh·kaht soo·trah
T-shirt	**kaos oblong**	kah·woss oh·blong
toy	**mainan**	mah·yee·nahn
woven mat [rug]	**tikar anyaman**	tee·kar ah·nyah·mahn
wood carvings	**ukiran kayu**	oo·kee·rahn kah·yoo

Indonesia is rich in craftsmanship tradition. Typical souvenirs include paintings, woven cloth, clothes, and wood carvings. Some of the oft-seen symbols of traditional Indonesian craftwork are the **Burung Garuda** (mythical Garuda bird), **wayang golek** (shadow theater puppets) and **keris** (traditional ceremonial knife with a blade shaped into waves).
Tourist spots such as Bali have plenty of stalls, shops or even entire villages dedicated to the showcasing of traditional art and craft.

Can I see this/that?	**Bisakah saya lihat ini/itu?** *bee·sah·kah sah·yah lee·haht ee·nee/ee·too*
It's in the window.	**Yang ada di jendela.** *yahng ah·dah dee jən·de·lah*
It's in the display case.	**Yang ada di kotak pajangan.** *yahng ah·dah dee koh·tahk pah·jah·ngahn*
I'd like…	**Saya mau…** *sah·yah mah·woo*
a (chain) bracelet	**gelang** *gə·lahng*
a (hoop) bracelet	**gelang kait** *gə·lahng kah·yeet*
a brooch	**bros** *bros*
earrings	**anting** *ahn·ting*
a necklace	**kalung** *kah·loong*
a ring	**cincin** *chin·chin*
a watch	**jam tangan** *jahm tah·ngahn*
copper	**tembaga** *təm·bah·gah*
crystal	**kristal** *kris·tahl*
diamonds	**intan** *in·tahn*
white/yellow gold	**emas putih/kuning** *ə·mahs poo·teeh/koo·ning*
pearls	**mutiara** *moo·tee·yah·rah*
platinum	**platinum** *plah·tee·noom*
sterling silver	**perak murni** *pe·rahk moor·nee*
Is this real?	**Ini asli?** *ee·nee ahs·lee*
Can you engrave it?	**Bisa anda gravir?** *bee·sah ahn·dah grah·veer*

Sport & Leisure

ESSENTIAL

When's the game?	**Kapan permainan mulai?** *kah•pahn pər•mah•yee•nahn moo•lye*
Where's the...?	**...di mana?** *dee•mah•nah*
beach	**pantai** *pahn•tye*
park	**taman** *tah•mahn*
pool	**kolam renang** *koh•lahm rə•nahng*
Is it safe to swim here?	**Apakah aman berenang di sini?** *ah•pah•kah ah•mahn bə•rə•nahng dee see•nee*
Can I rent [hire] golf clubs?	**Bisakah saya sewa peralatan golf?** *bee•sah•kah sah•yah seh•wah pə•rah•lah•tahn golf*
How much per hour?	**Berapa biayanya per jam?** *bə•rah•pah bee•yah•yah•nyah pər jahm*
How far is it to...?	**Seberapa jauh ke...?** *sə•bə•rah•pah jah•wooh kə*
Show me on the map, please.	**Tolong tunjukkan pada peta.** *toh•long toon•joo•kahn pah•dah pə•tah*

Watching Sport

When's the...game?	**Kapan permainan...?**	*kah·pahn pər·mah·yee·nahn*
When's the...match/	**Kapan pertandingan...?**	
race?		*kah·pahn pər·tahn·dee·ngahn*
badminton	**badminton** *bahd·min·ton*	
baseball	**bisbol** *bis·bol*	
basketball	**basket** *bahs·ket*	
boxing	**tinju** *teen·joo*	
cricket	**kriket** *kree·keht*	
cycling	**balap sepeda** *bah·lahp sə·peh·dah*	
golf	**golf** *golf*	
ping-pong	**ping-pong** *ping·pong*	
[table tennis]		
martial arts	**silat** *see·laht*	
soccer [football]	**sepak bola** *seh·pahk bo·lah*	
tennis	**tenis** *teh·nis*	
volleyball	**voli** *voh·lee*	
wrestling	**gulat** *goo·laht*	
Who's playing?	**Siapa yang main?** *see·yah·pah yahng mah·yeen*	
Where's the	**Arena balap/stadion di mana?**	
racetrack/stadium?	*ah·reh·nah bah·lahp/stah·dee·yon dee·mah·nah*	
Where can I place	**Di mana saya bisa taruhan?**	
a bet?	*dee mah·nah sah·yah bee·sah tah·roo·hahn*	

For Numbers, see page 169.

Playing Sport

Where is/are...?	**...di mana?** *dee·mah·nah*	
the golf course	**lapangan golf** *lah·pah·ngahn golf*	
the gym	**gym** *gym*	
the park	**taman** *tah·mahn*	
the tennis courts	**lapangan tenis** *lah·pah·ngahn teh·nis*	

Soccer (**sepak bola**) and badminton are the 'national' sports, and they have the largest following everywhere in Indonesia. **Sepak takraw**, a game that is a cross between volleyball and soccer, is also very popular. **Pencak silat**, a centuries-old Indonesian martial art, is both a sport and a form of artistic performance in West Java and West Sumatra. **Silat** displays are common at weddings and other cultural events.

How much per…?	**Berapa biayanya per…?**	bə·rah·pah bee·yah·yah·nyah pər
day	**hari**	hah·ree
hour	**jam**	jahm
game	**permainan**	pər·mah·yee·nahn
round	**babak**	bah·bahk
Can I hire…?	**Bisakah saya sewa…?**	bee·sah·kah sah·yah seh·wah
golf clubs	**peralatan golf**	pə·rah·lah·tahn golf
equipment	**perlengkapan**	pər·ləng·kah·pahn
a racket	**raket**	rah·ket

At the Beach/Pool

Where's the beach?	**Pantai di mana ?**	pahn·tye dee·mah·nah
Where's the pool?	**Kolam renang di mana?**	koh·lahm rə·nahng dee·mah·nah
Is there a…?	**Apakah ada…?**	ah·pah·kah ah·dah
kiddie pool	**kolam renang anak**	koh·lahm rə·nahng ah·nahk
indoor pool	**kolam renang dalam ruangan**	koh·lahm rə·nahng dah·lahm roo·wah·ngan
lifeguard	**penjaga**	pən·jah·gah

Is it safe...?	**Apakah aman...?** *ah-pah-kah ah-mahn*
to swim	**untuk berenang** *oon-took bə-rə-nahng*
to dive	**untuk menyelam** *oon-took mə-nya-lahm*
for children	**untuk anak-anak** *oon-took ah-nahk-ah-nahk*
I'd like to hire...	**Saya ingin menyewa...** *sah-yah ee-ngin mə-nyeh-wah*
a deck chair	**kursi pantai** *koor-see pahn-tye*
diving equipment	**perlengkapan menyelam** *pər-ləng-kah-pahn mə-nya-lahm*
a jet ski	**jet ski** *jet ski*
a motorboat	**perahu motor** *pə-rah-hoo moh-tor*
a rowboat	**perahu dayung** *pə-rah-hoo dah-yoong*
snorkeling equipment	**perlengkapan snorkeling** *pər-ləng-kah-pahn snorkeling*
a surfboard	**papan selancar** *pah-pahn sə-lahn-chahr*
a towel	**handuk** *hahn-dook*
an umbrella	**payung** *pah-yoong*
water skis	**ski air** *ski ah-yeer*
a windsurfer	**selancar angin** *sə-lahn-chahr ah-ngin*
For...hours.	**Selama...jam.** *sə-lah-mah...jahm*

Out in the Country

A map of…, please.	**Tolong minta peta…** *toh·long min·tah pə·tah*
this region/district	**wilayah/distrik ini** *wee·lah·yah/dis·trik ee·nee*
the walking routes	**rute jalan kaki** *roo·tə jah·lahn kah·kee*
the bike routes	**rute sepeda** *roo·tə sə·peh·dah*
the trails	**lintas alam** *lin·tahs ah·lahm*
Is it…?	**Apakah…?** *ah·pah·kah*
easy	**mudah** *moo·dah*
difficult	**sulit** *soo·lit*
far	**jauh** *jah·wooh*
steep	**terjal** *tər·jahl*
How far is it to…?	**Seberapa jauh ke…?** *sə·bə·rah·pah jah·wooh kə*
Show me on the map, please.	**Tolong tunjukkan pada peta.** *toh·long toon·joo·kahn pah·dah pə·tah*
I'm lost.	**Saya kesasar.** *sah·yah kə·sah·sar*
Where's the…?	**…di mana?** *dee·mah·nah*
bridge	**jembatan** *jəm·bah·tahn*
cave	**gua** *goo·wah*
cliff	**jurang** *joo·rahng*
desert	**gurun** *goo·roon*

farm (large/small)	**pertanian/perkebunan**	pər·tah·nee·yahn/ pər·kə·boo·nahn
field	**lapangan/ladang**	lah·pah·ngahn/lah·dahng
forest	**hutan**	hoo·tahn
hill	**bukit**	boo·kit
lake	**danau**	dah·now
mountain	**gunung**	goo·noong
nature preserve	**cagar alam**	chah·gar ah·lahm
overlook [viewpoint]	**titik pandang**	tee·tik pahn·dahng
park	**taman**	tah·mahn
path	**jalur**	jah·loor
peak	**puncak**	poon·chahk
picnic area	**area piknik**	ah·reh·yah pik·nik
pond	**kolam**	koh·lahm
river	**sungai**	soo·ngay
sea	**laut**	lah·woot
hot spring	**mata air panas**	mah·tah ah·eer pah·nahs
stream	**kali/sungai kecil**	kah·lee/soo·ngay kə·cheel
valley	**lembah**	ləm·bah
vineyard	**kebun anggur**	kə·boon ahng·goor
waterfall	**air terjun**	ah·yeer tər·joon

Going Out

ESSENTIAL

What's there to do at night?	**Apa yang dilakukan di waktu malam?** *ah•pah yahng dee•lah•koo•kahn dee wahk•too mah•lahm*
Do you have a program of events?	**Anda punya program acara?** *ahn•dah poo•nyah pro•grahm ah•chah•rah*
What's playing tonight?	**Apa yang diputar malam ini?** *ah•pah yahng dee•poo•tar mah•lahm ee•nee*
Where's the...?	**...di mana?** *dee•mah•nah*
downtown area	**pusat kota** *poo•saht koh•tah*
bar	**bar** *bar*
dance club	**klub dansa** *kloob dahn•sah*
Is there a cover charge?	**Apakah ada cover charge?** *ah•pah•kah ah•dah cover charge*

Entertainment

Can you recommend…?	**Bisa anda menyarankan…?** *bee·sah ahn·dah mə·nyah·rahn·kahn*
a concert	**konser** *kon·ser*
a movie	**film** *film*
an opera	**opera** *o·pə·rah*
a play	**sandiwara** *sahn·dee·wah·rah*
When does it start/end?	**Kapan mulai/selesai?** *kah·pahn moo·lye/sə·lə·sye*
Where's the…?	**…di mana?** *dee·mah·nah*
concert hall	**aula konser** *ah·woo·lah kon·ser*
opera house	**gedung opera** *gə·doong o·pə·rah*
movie theater	**bioskop** *bee·yos·kop*
theater	**teater** *teh·yah·tər*
What's the dress code?	**Apakah ada aturan busana?** *ah·pah·kah ah·dah ah·too·rahn boo·sah·nah*
I like…music.	**Saya suka musik…** *sah·yah soo·kah moo·sik*
classical	**klasik** *klah·sik*
folk	**musik rakyat** *moo·sik rahk·yaht*
jazz	**jazz** *jazz*
pop	**pop** *pop*
rap	**rap** *rap*

YOU MAY HEAR…

Tolong matikan ponsel anda.
toh·long mah·teekan pon·sel ahn·dah

Turn off your cell [mobile] phones, please.

Nightlife

What's there to do at night?	**Apa yang dilakukan di waktu malam?** *ah·pah yahng dee·lah·koo·kahn dee wahk·too mah·lahm*
Can you recommend...?	**Bisa anda menyarankan...?** *bee·sah ahn·dah mə·nyah·rahn·kahn*
a bar	**bar** *bar*
a casino	**kasino** *kah·see·noh*
a dance club	**klub dansa** *kloob dahn·sah*
a gay club	**klub penyuka sesama jenis** *kloob pə·nyoo·kah sə·sah·mah jə·nees*
a jazz club	**klub jazz** *kloob jazz*
a club with Indonesian music	**klub dengan musik Indonesia** *kloob deh·ngan moo·sik in·doh·neh·shah*
Is there live music?	**Apakah ada pertunjukan musik hidup?** *ah·pah·kah ah·dah pər·toon·joo·kahn moo·sik hee·doop*
How do I get there?	**Bagaimana saya ke sana?** *bah·gye·mah·nah sah·yah kə sah·nah*
Is there a cover charge?	**Apakah ada cover charge?** *ah·pah·kah ah·dah cover charge*
Let's go dancing.	**Ayo kita dansa.** *ah·yoh kee·tah dahn·sah*
Is this area safe at night?	**Apa daerah ini aman di waktu malam?** *ah·pah dah·eh·rah ee·nee ah·mahn dee wahk·too mah·lahm*

Pubs, discos and karaoke lounges are popular nightlife spots. The major cities and beach resorts have nightclubs and cocktail lounges with live music. The best nightlife is in the capital Jakarta and tourist spots such as Bali. Club crowds swell after 11:00pm or midnight, and there is a cover charge on Friday and Saturday, which usually includes a drink. During the Muslim fasting month of Ramadan, all types of nightlife close by midnight. Some even close for the entire duration of Ramadan.

Special Requirements

Business Travel

ESSENTIAL

I'm here on business.	**Saya di sini untuk urusan bisnis.** *sah•yah dee see•nee oon•took oo•roo•sahn biss•niss*
Here's my business card.	**Ini kartu nama saya.** *ee•nee kahr•too nah•mah sah•yah*
Can I have your card?	**Boleh minta kartu nama anda?** *bo•leh min•tah kahr•too nah•mah ahn•dah*
I have a meeting with…	**Saya ada rapat dengan…** *sah•yah ah•dah rah•paht də•ngahn*
Where's the…?	**…di mana?** *dee•mah•nah*
business center	**pusat bisnis** *poo•saht biss•niss*
convention hall	**aula konvensi** *ah•woo•lah kon•ven•see*
meeting room	**ruang rapat** *roo•wahng rah•paht*

On Business

I'm here for a conference.	**Saya disini untuk konferensi.** *sah•yah dee•see•nee oon•took kon•fə•ren•see*
I'm here for a seminar.	**Saya disini untuk seminar.** *sah•yah dee•see•nee oon•took sə•mee•nar*
I'm here for a meeting.	**Saya di sini untuk rapat.** *sah•yah dee see•nee oon•took rah•paht*
My name is…	**Nama saya…** *nah•mah sah•yah*
May I introduce my colleague…	**Bisa saya perkenalkan rekan saya…** *bee•sah sah•yah pər•kə•nahl•kahn rə•kahn sah•yah*
I have a meeting with…	**Saya ada rapat dengan…** *sah•yah ah•dah rah•paht də•ngahn*

When presenting or receiving a business card in Indonesia, hold the card in the right hand or with both hands. If you have just received a card, do not put it away before reading the card. Receiving anything using the left hand is considered rude. Use the right hand, even if you are left-handed.

Indonesian first names appear at the start of the person's full name. Therefore, 'Mohammed Ali bin Abdullah' would be called 'Mohammed Ali' (his first name) by his colleagues. Take note that Indonesian last names do not function in quite the same way as English last names. The person in our example here would be referred to as 'Mr Mohammed Ali', and not 'Mr Abdullah' by his business contacts.

Ethnic Chinese in Indonesia generally use Indonesian names.

I have an appointment with…	**Saya ada janji dengan…**	sah•yah ah•dah jahn•jee də•ngahn
I'm sorry I'm late.	**Maaf, saya terlambat.**	mah•ahf, sah•yah tər•lahm•baht
I need an interpreter.	**Saya butuh penerjemah.**	sah•yah boo•tooh pə•nər•jə•mah

YOU MAY HEAR...

Anda sudah buat janji?
ahn·dah soo·dah boo·waht jahn·jee

Do you have an appointment?

Dengan siapa? *də·ngahn see·yah·pah*

With whom?

Dia sedang rapat.
dee·yah sə·dahng rah·paht

He/She is in a meeting.

Mohon tunggu sebentar.
mo·hon toong·goo sə·ben·tar

One moment, please.

Silakan duduk.
see·lah·kahn doo·dook

Have a seat.

Anda mau minum apa?
ahn·dah mah·woo mee·noom ah·pah

Would you like something to drink?

Terima kasih telah datang.
tə·ree·mah kah·seeh tə·lah dah·tahng

Thank you for coming.

You can reach me at the...Hotel.	**Anda bisa menghubungi saya di Hotel...** *ahn·dah bee·sah məng·hoo·boo·ngee sah·yah dee hoh·tel...*
I'm here until...	**Saya di sini sampai...** *sah·yah dee see·nee sahm·pye*
I need to...	**Saya perlu...** *sah·yah pər·loo*
make a call	**menelepon** *mə·nə·lə·pon*
make a photocopy	**membuat fotokopi** *mam·boo·waht foh·toh·koh·pee*
send an e-mail	**kirim e-mail** *kee·rim e-mail*
send a fax	**kirim faks** *kee·rim feks*
send a package (overnight)	**kirim paket (satu malam sampai)** *kee·rim pah·ket (sah·too mah·lahm sahm·pye)*
It was a pleasure to to meet you.	**Senang berkenalan dengan anda.** *sə·nahng bər·kə·nah·lahn də·ngahn ahn·dah*

For Communications, see page 52.

ESSENTIAL

Is there a discount for kids?	**Apakah ada diskon untuk anak kecil?** *ah·pah·kah ah·dah dis·kon oon·took ah·nahk kə·cheel*
Can you recommend a babysitter?	**Bisakah anda menyarankan penjaga bayi?** *bee·sah·kah ahn·dah mə·nyah·rahn·kahn pən·jah·gah bah·yee*
Do you have a child's seat?	**Ada kursi untuk anak kecil?** *ah·dah koor·see oon·took ah·nahk kə·cheel*
Do you have a child's highchair?	**Ada kursi tinggi untuk anak kecil?** *ah·dah koor·see ting·gee oon·took ah·nahk kə·cheel*
Where can I change the baby?	**Di mana saya bisa mengganti popok bayi?** *Dee mah·nah sah·yah bee·sah məng·gahn·tee poh·pok bah·yee?*

Out & About

Can you recommend something for kids?	**Bisakah anda menyarankan sesuatu untuk anak kecil?** *bee·sah·kah ahn·dah mə·nyah·rahn·kahn sə·soo·wah·too oon·took ah·nahk kə·cheel*
Where's the…?	**…di mana?** *dee·mah·nah*
amusement park	**taman hiburan** *tah·mahn hee·boo·rahn*
arcade	**arena bermain** *ah·reh·nah bər·mah·yeen*
kiddie [paddling] pool	**kolam renang anak** *koh·lahm rə·nahng ah·nahk*
park	**taman** *tah·mahn*
playground	**taman bermain** *tah·mahn bər·mah·yeen*
zoo	**kebun binatang** *kə·boon bee·nah·tahng*

Are kids allowed?	**Apakah anak kecil bisa masuk?** *ah·pah·kah ah·nahk kə·cheel bee·sah mah·sook*
Is it safe for kids?	**Apakah aman untuk anak kecil?** *ah·pah·kah ah·mahn oon·took ah·nahk kə·cheel*
Is it suitable for... year olds?	**Apakah cocok untuk umur...tahun?** *ah·pah·kah cho·chok oon·took oo·moor...tah·hoon*

For Numbers, see page 169.

Baby Essentials

Do you have...?	**Apakah anda punya...?** *ah·pah·kah ahn·dah poo·nyah*
a baby bottle	**botol bayi** *boh·tol bah·yee*
baby food	**makanan bayi** *mah·kah·nahn bah·yee*
baby wipes	**penyeka untuk bayi** *pə·nyeh·kah oon·took bah·yee*
a car seat	**kursi mobil** *koor·see moh·beel*
a children's menu/portion	**menu/porsi untuk anak kecil** *meh·noo/por·see oon·took ah·nahk kə·cheel*
a child's seat/ highchair	**tempat duduk/kursi tinggi anak kecil** *təm·paht doo·dook/koor·see ting·gee ah·nahk kə·cheel*
a crib/cot	**buaian/tempat tidur bayi** *boo·wye·yahn/təm·paht tee·door bah·yee*

diapers [nappies]	**popok** *poh•pok*
formula [baby food]	**susu formula** *soo•soo for•moo•lah*
a pacifier [dummy]	**dot bayi** *dot bah•yee*
a playpen	**tempat bayi bermain** *tem•path bah•yee ber•mah•yeen*
a stroller [pushchair]	**kursi untuk belajar jalan** *koor•see oon•took bə•lah•jar jah•lahn*
Can I breastfeed the baby here?	**Bisa saya menyusui bayi di sini?** *bee•sah sah•yah mə•nyoo•soo•wee bah•yee dee see•nee*
Where can I breastfeed the baby?	**Di mana saya bisa menyusui bayi?** *dee mah•nah sah•yah bee•sah mə•nyoo•soo•wee bah•yee*
Where can I change the baby?	**Di mana saya bisa mengganti popok bayi?** *dee mah•nah sah•yah bee•sah məng•gahn•tee poh•pok bah•yee*

YOU MAY HEAR...

Aduh lucunya! *ah•dooh loo•choo•nyah*	How cute!
Siapa namanya? *see•yah•pah nah•mah•nyah*	What's his/her name?
Berapa usianya? *bə•rah•pah oo•see•yah•nyah*	How old is he/she?

Babysitting

| Can you recommend a babysitter? | **Bisakah anda menyarankan penjaga bayi?** *bee•sah•kah ahn•dah mə•nyah•rahn•kahn pən•jah•gah bah•yee* |
| What do you/they charge? | **Berapa biayanya?** *bə•rah•pah bee•yah•yah•nyah* |

I'll be back by...	**Saya akan kembali jam...** *sah·yah ah·kahn kəm·bah·lee jahm*
I can be reached at...	**Saya bisa dihubungi di...** *sah·yah bee·sah dee·hoo·boo·ngee dee*

Health & Emergency

Can you recommend a pediatrician?	**Bisakah anda menyarankan dokter anak?** *bee·sah·kah ahn·dah mə·nyah·rahn·kahn dok·tər ah·nahk*
My child is allergic to...	**Anak saya alergi...** *ah·nahk sah·yah ah·ler·gee*
My child is missing.	**Anak saya hilang.** *ah·nahk sah·yah hee·lahng*
Have you seen a boy?	**Anda ada melihat anak kecil laki-laki?** *ahn·dah ah·dah mə·lee·haht ah·nahk kə·cheel lah·kee·lah·kee*
Have you seen a girl?	**Anda ada melihat anak kecil perempuan?** *ahn·dah ah·dah mə·lee·haht ah·nahk kə·cheel pə·rəm·poo·wahn*

ESSENTIAL

Is there...?	**Apakah ada...?** *ah·pah·kah ah·dah*
access for the disabled	**jalan untuk penyandang cacat** *jah·lahn oon·took pa·nyahn·dahng chah·chaht*
a wheelchair ramp	**jalan untuk kursi roda** *jah·lahn oon·took koor·see roh·dah*
a handicapped-[disabled-] accessible toilet	**kamar kecil untuk penyandang cacat** *kah·mar ka·cheel oon·took pa·nyahn·dahng chah·chaht*
I need...	**Saya perlu** *sah·yah par·loo*
assistance	**bantuan** *bahn·too·wahn*
an elevator [a lift]	**lift** *lift*
a ground-floor room	**kamar di lantai dasar** *kah·mar dee lahn·tye dah·sar*

Asking for Assistance

I'm...	**Saya...** *sah·yah*
disabled	**cacat** *chah·chaht*
visually impaired	**tidak bisa melihat jelas** *tee·dahk bee·sah ma·lee·haht ja·lahs*
hearing impaired/ deaf/dumb	**tidak bisa mendengar/tuli/bisu** *tee·dahk bee·sah man·da·ngahr/too·lee/bee·soo*
unable to walk far	**tidak bisa berjalan jauh** *tee·dahk bee·sah bar·jah·lahn jah·wooh*
unable to use the stairs	**tidak dapat naik-turun tangga** *tee·dahk dah·paht nah·yeek·too·roon tahng·gah*

Please speak louder.	**Tolong bicara lebih keras.** *toh·long bee·chah·rah la·beeh ka·rahs*
Can I bring my wheelchair?	**Bisakah saya membawa kursi roda?** *bee·sa·kah sah·yah mam·bah·wah koor·see ro·dah*
Are guide dogs permitted?	**Apakah anjing pemandu diizinkan?** *ah·pah·kah ahn·jeeng pa·mahn·doo dee·ee·zin·kahn*
Can you help me?	**Bisa bantu saya?/Bisa tolong saya?** *bee·sah bahn·too sah·yah/bee·sah toh·long sah·yah*
Please open/hold the door.	**Tolong buka/tahan pintunya.** *toh·long boo·kah/tah·hahn pin·too·nyah*

In an Emergency

Emergencies

ESSENTIAL

Help!	**Tolong!** *toh·long*
Go away!	**Pergi sana!** *pər·gee sah·nah*
Stop, thief!	**Stop, pencuri!** *stop, pən·choo·ree*
Get a doctor!	**Panggil dokter!** *pahng·geel dok·tər*
Fire!	**Kebakaran!** *kə·bah·kah·rahn*
I'm lost.	**Saya kesasar.** *sah·yah kə·sah·sar*
Can you help me?	**Bisa bantu saya/Bisa tolong saya?** *bee·sah bahn·too sah·yah/bee·sah toh·long sah·yah*

In an emergency, dial: **110** for the police; **113** for the fire brigade; **118** for the ambulance; and **115** for the search and rescue team.

YOU MAY HEAR...

Isi formulir ini.
ee·see for·moo·leer ee·nee

Fill out this form.

Tolong tanda pengenal anda.
toh·long tahn·dah pə·ngə·nahl ahn·dah

Your identification, please.

Kapan/Di mana kejadiannya?
kah·pahn/dee mah·nah keh·jah·dee·yan·nyah

When/Where did it happen?

Orangnya seperti apa?
oh·rahng·nyah sə·pər·tee ah·pah

What does he/she look like?

Police

ESSENTIAL

Call the police!	**Panggil polisi!** *pahng·geel poh·lee·see*
Where's the police station?	**Kantor polisi di mana?** *kahn·tor poh·lee·see dee mah·nah*
There was an accident/an attack.	**Ada kecelakaan/serangan.** *ah·dah kə·chə·lah·kah·ahn/sə·rah·ngahn*
My child is missing.	**Anak saya hilang.** *ah·nahk sah·yah hee·lahng*
I need...	**Saya perlu** *sah·yah pər·loo*
an interpreter	**penerjemah** *pə·nər·jə·mah*
to contact my lawyer	**menghubungi pengacara saya** *məng·hoo·boo·ngee pə·ngah·chah·rah sah·yah*
to make a phone call	**menelepon** *mə·nə·lə·pon*
I'm innocent.	**Saya tidak bersalah.** *sah·yah tee·dahk bər·sah·lah*

Crime & Lost Property

I want to report...	**Saya ingin melaporkan...** *sah·yah ee·ngin mə·lah·por·kahn*
a mugging	**penjambretan** *pən·jahm·bre·tahn*
a rape	**pemerkosaan** *pər·mer·ko·sah·ahn*
a theft	**pencurian** *pən·choo·ree·yahn*
I was mugged/robbed.	**Saya dijambret/dirampok.** *sah·yah dee·jahm·bret/dee·rahm·pok*
I lost my...	**Saya kehilangan...** *sah·yah kə·hee·lah·ngahn*
My...was stolen.	**...saya dicuri.** *sah·yah dee·choo·ree*
backpack	**ransel** *rahn·səl*
bicycle	**sepeda** *sə·peh·dah*

camera	**kamera** *kah•meh•rah*
(hire) car	**mobil (sewa)** *moh•beel (seh•wah)*
computer	**komputer** *kom•poo•tər*
credit card	**kartu kredit** *kar•too kreh•dit*
jewelry	**perhiasan** *pər•hee•yah•sahn*
money	**uang** *oo•wahng*
passport	**paspor** *pahs•por*
handbag	**tas tangan** *tahs tah•ngahn*
traveler's checks	**cek wisata** *check wee•sah•tah*
wallet/purse	**dompet/tas kecil** *dom•pet/tahs kə•cheel*
I need a police report.	**Saya perlu laporan polisi.** *sah•yah pər•loo lah•poh•rahn po•lee•see*
Where is the British/American/Irish embassy?	**Di mana letak Kedubes Inggris/Amerika/Irlandia?** *dee mah•nah lə•tahk Kə•doo•behs ing•grees/Ah•meh•ree•kah/Ir•lahn•dee•ah*

ESSENTIAL

I'm sick [ill].	**Saya sakit.** *sah•yah sah•kit*
I need an English-speaking doctor.	**Saya perlu dokter yang dapat berbahasa Inggris.** *sah•yah pər•loo dok•tər yahng dah•paht bər•bah•hah•sah ing•grees*
It hurts here.	**Sakit di sini.** *sah•kit dee see•nee*
I have a stomachache.	**Saya sakit perut.** *sah•yah sah•kit pə•root*

Finding a Doctor

Can you recommend a doctor/dentist?	**Bisakah anda menyarankan dokter/dokter gigi?** *bee•sah•kah ahn•dah mə•nyah•rahn•kahn dok•tar/dok•tar gee•gee*
Can the doctor come here?	**Apakah dokternya bisa datang ke sini?** *ah•pah•kah dok•tərnya bee•sah dah•tahng kə see•nee*
I need an English-speaking doctor.	**Saya perlu dokter yang dapat berbahasa Inggris.** *sah•yah pər•loo dok•tər yahng dah•paht bər•bah•hah•sah ing•grees*
What are the office hours?	**Bukanya jam berapa?** *boo•kah•nyah jahm bə•rah•pah*
I'd like an appointment for...	**Kapan jam kantornya buka?** *kah•pahn jahm kahn•tohr•nyah boo•kha*
today	**hariini** *hah•ri ee•nee*
tomorrow	**besok** *beh•sok*
as soon as possible	**secepatnya** *sə•chə•paht•nyah*
It's urgent.	**Ini mendesak.** *ee•nee mən•də•sahk*

Symptoms

I'm...	**Saya...** *sah•yah*
bleeding	**mengalami perdarahan** *mə•ngah•lah•mee pər•dah•rah•hahn*
constipated	**sembelit** *səm•bə•lit*
dizzy	**pusing** *poo•sing*
nauseous	**mual** *moo•wahl*
vomiting	**muntah-muntah** *moon•tah•moon•tah*
It hurts here.	**Sakit di sini.** *sah•kit dee see•nee*
I have...	**Saya ada...** *sah•yah ah•dah*
an allergic reaction	**suka alergi** *soo•kah ah•ler•gee*
chest pain	**sakit dada** *sah•kit dah•dah*
menstrual cramps	**kejang kalau haid** *kə•jahng kah•low hah•yeed*
diarrhea	**diare** *dee•yah•reh*
an earache	**sakit telinga** *sah•kit tə•lee•ngah*
a fever	**demam** *də•mahm*
pain	**kesakitan** *kə•sah•kee•tahn*
a rash	**gatal-gatal** *gah•tahl•gah•tahl*
some swelling	**bengkak** *bəng•kahk*
a sore throat	**sakit tenggorokan** *sah•kit təng•goh•roh•kahn*
a stomachache	**sakit perut** *sah•kit pə•root*

sunstroke	**sengatan matahari** *sə·ngah·tahn mah·tah·hah·ree*
I have a sprain.	**Saya keseleo.** *sah·yah kə·sə·leh·yoh*
I've been sick [ill] for...days.	**Saya sakit sudah...hari.** *sah·yah sah·kit soo·dah...hah·ree*

Conditions

I'm anemic.	**Saya anemia.** *sah·yah ah·neh·mee·yah*
I have epilepsy	**Saya menderita epilepsi.** *sah·yah mən·də·ree·tah eh·pi·lehp·see*
I'm allergic to antibiotics/penicillin.	**Saya alergi terhadap antibiotik/penisilin.** *sah·yah ah·ler·gee tər·hah·dahp ahn·tee·bee·yo·tik/ peh·nee·see·lin*
I have...	**Saya ada...** *sah·yah ah·dah*
arthritis	**peradangan sendi** *pə·rah·dah·ngahn sən·dee*
asthma	**asthma** *ahs·mah*
a heart condition	**sakit jantung** *sah·kit jahn·toong*
diabetes	**diabetes** *dee·yah·beh·təs*
high/low blood pressure	**tekanan darah tinggi/rendah** *tə·kah·nahn dah·rah ting·gee/rən·dah*
I'm on (medication)...	**Saya sedang dalam (pengobatan)...** *sah·yah sə·dahng dah·lahm (pə·ngo·bah·tahn)*

Treatment

Do I need a prescription medicine?	**Apakah saya perlu resep dokter/obat?** *ah·pah·kah sah·yah pər·loo rə·sep dok·tər/oh·baht*
Can you prescribe a generic drug [medication]?	**Bisa tolong beri resep obat generik?** *bee·sah to·long bə·ree rə·sep oh·baht geh·neh·rik*
Where can I get it?	**Di mana saya bisa memperolehnya?** *dee mah·nah sah·yah bee·sah məm·pər·oh·leh·nyah*
Is this over the counter?	**Apakah ini bisa dibeli bebas?** *ah·pah·kah ee·nee bee·sah dee·bə·lee beh·bahs*

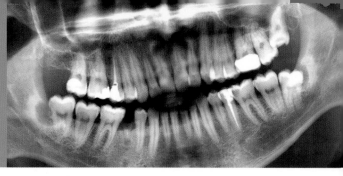

Hospital

Notify my family, please.	**Tolong beritahu keluarga saya.** *toh·long bə·ree·tah·hoo kə·loo·wahr·gah sah·yah*
I'm in pain.	**Saya kesakitan.** *sah·yah kə·sah·kee·tahn*
I need a doctor/nurse.	**Saya perlu dokter/perawat.** *sah·yah pər·loo dok·tər/pə·rah·what*
When are visiting hours?	**Kapan jam kunjungan pasien?** *kah·pahn jahm koon·joo·ngahn pah·see·yen*
I'm visiting...	**Saya mengunjungi...** *sah·yah mə·ngoon·joo·ngee*

Dentist

I have a broken tooth.	**Gigi saya patah.** *gee·gee sah·yah pah·tah*
I have lost a filling.	**Tambalan gigi saya lepas.** *tahm·bah·lahn gee·gee sah·yah lepas*
I have a toothache.	**Saya sakit gigi.** *sah·yah sah·kit gee·gee*
Can you fix this denture?	**Bisa anda perbaiki gigi palsu ini?** *bee·sah ahn·dah pər·bah·yee·kee gee·gee pahl·soo ee·nee*

Gynecologist

I have cramps.	**Saya menderita kejang.** *sah·yah mən·də·ree·tah kə·jahng*
I have a vaginal infection.	**Vagina saya infeksi.** *vah·gee·nah sah·yah in·fek·see*

YOU MAY HEAR...

Apa yang sakit? *ah·pah yahng sah·kit* — What's wrong?

Rasa sakitnya di mana? *rah·sah sah·kit·nyah dee mah·nah* — Where does it hurt?

Apakah di sini sakit? *ah·pah·kah dee see·nee sah·kit* — Does it hurt here?

Apakah anda sedang dalam pengobatan? *ah·pah·kah ahn·dah sə·dahng dah·lahm pə·ngo·bah·tahn* — Are you on medication?

Apakah anda alergi terhadap sesuatu? *ah·pah·kah ahn·dah ah·ler·gee tər·hah·dahp sə·soo·wah·too* — Are you allergic to anything?

Buka mulut anda. *boo·kah moo·loot ahn·dah* — Open your mouth.

Tarik napas panjang. *tah·reek nah·pahs pahn·jahng* — Breathe deeply.

Coba batuk. *cho·bah bah·took.* — Cough please.

Periksa ke spesialis. *pə·rik·sah kə speh·shah·lis* — See a specialist.

Pergi ke rumah sakit. *pər·gee kə roo·mah sah·kit* — Go to the hospital.

Itu/Ini... *ee·too/ee·nee* — It's...

    patah *pah·tah* — broken

    menular *me·noo·lar* — contagious

    terinfeksi *tər·in·fek·see* — infected

    terkilir *tər·kee·lir* — sprained

    tidak apa-apa/tidak parah *tee·dahk ah·pah·ah·pah/tee·dahk pah·rah* — nothing serious

---

I missed my period.   **Haid saya tidak datang.** *hah·yee sah·yah tee·dahk dah·tahng*

I'm on the Pill.	**Saya minum Pil KB.** *sah·yah mee·noom pil kah·beh*
I'm (...months) pregnant.	**Saya hamil (...bulan).** *sah·yah hah·mill (...boo·lahn)*
I'm not pregnant.	**Saya tidak hamil.** *sah·yah tee·dahk hah·mill*
My last period was...	**Haid saya yang terakhir...** *hah·yeed sah·yah yahng tər·ah·khir*

Optician

I lost...	**Saya kehilangan...** *sah·yah kə·hee·lah·ngahn*
a contact lens	**lensa kontak** *len·sah kon·tahk*
my glasses	**kacamata** *kah·chah·mah·tah*
a lens	**lensa** *len·sah*

Payment & Insurance

How much?	**Berapa biayanya?** *bə·rah·pah bee·yah·yah·nyah*
Can I pay by credit card?	**Bisa saya bayar pakai kartu kredit?** *bee·sah sah·yah bah·yahr pah·kye kar·too kreh·dit*
I have insurance.	**Saya punya asuransi.** *sah·yah poo·nyah ah·soo·rahn·see*
I need a receipt for my insurance.	**Saya perlu tanda terima untuk asuransi saya.** *sah·yah pər·loo tahn·dah tə·ree·mah oon·took ah·soo·rahn·see sah·yah*

Pharmacy

ESSENTIAL

Where's the pharmacy?	**Apotek di mana?** *ah·po·teck dee mah·nah*
What time does it open/close?	**Jam berapa buka/tutup?** *jahm bə·rah·pah boo·kah/too·toop*
What would you recommend for…?	**Apa yang akan anda sarankan untuk…?** *ah·pah yahng ah·kahn ahn·dah sah·rahn·kahn oon·took*
How much do I take?	**Berapa yang harus saya minum?** *bə·rah·pah yahng hah·roos sah·yah mee·noom*
Can you fill [up] this prescription?	**Bisa tolong buatkan obat resep ini?** *bee·sah toh·long boo·waht·kahn oh·baht rə·sep ee·nee*
I'm allergic to…	**Saya alergi terhadap…** *sah·yah ah·ler·gee tər·hah·dahp*

What to Take

How much do I take?	**Berapa yang harus saya minum?** *bə·rah·pah yahng hah·roos sah·yah mee·noom*
How often?	**Seberapa sering?** *sə·bə·rah·pah sə·ring*
Is it safe for children?	**Apakah aman untuk anak kecil?** *ah·pah·kah ah·mahn oon·took ah·nahk kə·cheel*
I'm taking…	**Saya minum…** *sah·yah mee·noom*
Are there side effects?	**Apakah ada efek sampingan?** *ah·pah·kah ah·dah eh·fek sahm·pee·ngahn*
I need something for…	**Saya perlu sesuatu untuk…** *sah·yah pər·loo sə·soo·wah·too oon·took*
a cold	**flu** *flu*
a cough	**batuk** *bah·took*
diarrhea	**diare** *dee·yah·reh*

YOU MAY SEE...

TABLET *tahb·let*	tablet
TETES *teh·tes*	drop
SENDOK TEH *sen·dok teh*	teaspoon
SATU KALI/TIGA KALI SEHARI *sah·too kah·lee/tee·gah kah·lee sə·hah·ree*	once/three times a day
SETELAH/SEBELUM/SAAT MAKAN *sə·tə·lah/sə·bə·loom/ sah·aht mah·kahn*	after/before/with meals
SAAT PERUT KOSONG *sah·aht pə·root koh·song*	on an empty stomach
TELAN SEMUANYA *tə·lahn sə·moo·wahnya*	swallow whole
BISA MENYEBABKAN PUSING *bee·sah mə·nyə·bahb·kahn poo·sing*	may cause drowsiness
HANYA UNTUK BAGIAN LUAR *hah·nyah oon·took bah·gee·yahn loo·wahr*	for external use only

a fever	**demam** *də·mahm*	
a hangover	**teler** *teh·ler*	
insect bites	**gigitan serangga** *gee·gee·tahn sə·rahng·gah*	
sea sickness	**mabuk laut** *mah·book lah·woot*	
a sore throat	**sakit tenggorokan** *sah·kit tang·goh·roh·kahn*	
sunburn	**sengatan matahari** *sə·ngah·tahn mah·tah·hah·ree*	
a toothache	**sakit gigi** *sah·keet gee·gee*	
an upset stomach	**sakit perut** *sah·kit pə·root*	

Basic Supplies

I'd like...	**Saya perlu...** *sah·yah pər·loo*
acetaminophen	**acetaminophen** *acetaminophen*
aftershave lotion	**aftershave lotion** *aftershave lotion*
antiseptic cream	**krim antiseptik** *kreem ahn·tee·sehp·tik*
aspirin	**aspirin** *aspirin*
bandages	**perban** *pər·bahn*
a comb	**sisir** *see·seer*
condoms	**kondom** *kon·dom*
contact lens solution	**larutan lensa kontak** *lah·roo·tahn len·sah kon·tahk*
deodorant	**deodorant** *deodorant*
a hairbrush	**sikat rambut** *see·kaht rahm·boot*
hairspray	**hairspray** *hairspray*
ibuprofen	**ibuprofen** *ibuprofen*
insect repellent	**pengusir serangga** *pə·ngoo·seer sə·rahng·gah*
lotion	**lotion** *lotion*
a nail file	**gunting kuku** *goon·ting koo·koo*
a (disposable) razor	**silet cukur (sekali pakai)** *see·let choo·koor (sə·kah·lee pah·kye)*
razor blades	**pisau cukur** *pee·sow choo·koor*

sanitary napkins [towels]	**pembalut wanita** *pəm·bah·loot wah·nee·tah*
shampoo/ conditioner	**shampoo/conditioner** *shahm·poh/conditioner*
soap	**sabun** *sah·boon*
sunscreen	**tabir surya** *tah·beer soor·yah*
tampons	**tampon** *tahm·pon*
tissues	**tisu** *tee·soo*
toilet paper	**kertas WC** *kər·tahs weh·seh*
toothpaste	**pasta gigi** *pahs·tah gee·gee*

For Baby Essentials, see page 146.

Drinking tap water is not recommended in Indonesia. Avoid drinks served with ice as well. Most water served in restaurants will be boiled or purified and is thus safe for consumption. As a precaution, always drink boiled water, especially in rural areas. Bottled water and mineral water can be purchased in major towns.

It is important to drink sufficiently to avoid dehydration; drink more than you would normally if you are from a temperate country. Cooked food from most stalls is generally safe.

If you are visiting remote rainforest areas, it is advisable to take protection against malaria. See your doctor before leaving home. Malaria tablets are available without prescription in Indonesia at **Toko Obat** (drug store) or from an **Apotek** (pharmacy). Dengue fever is also a potential health risk.

Grammar

Sentence structure

The basic sentence structure in the Indonesian language is similar to English, subject-verb-object. Examples:

I sleep. **Saya tidur.**

You are pretty. **Anda cantik.**

I drink tea. **Saya minum teh.**

He wants to eat rice. **Dia ingin makan nasi.**

There are no equivalents of the English articles 'a', 'an' and 'the', and auxiliary verbs like 'is', 'are', 'am' in Indonesian.

Pronouns

Personal pronouns in Indonesian are:

I	**saya** *sah·yah* (formal),	**aku** *ah·koo* (informal)	
you	**anda** *ahn·dah* (formal),	**kau/kamu** *kow/kah·moo* (informal)	
he/she	**dia** *dee·ah*		
we	**kami** *kah·mee* (exclusive),	**kita** *kee·tah* (inclusive)	
you (plural)	**kalian** *kah·lee·ahn*		
they	**mereka** *mə·reh·kah*		

Possessive pronouns are formed by putting the pronouns after a noun:

My key **Kunci saya**

Your key **Kunci anda**

Word formation

Many Indonesian words are formed by adding prefixes and suffixes to base words. These affixations are used to change the nature of the base word, and sometimes they even change the meaning of the word. The most common affixes are described below.

Noun affixes are used to form new nouns:

Type	Affix	Root word	Derived word
Prefix	pe-	**curi** (steal)	**pencuri** (thief, one who steals)
Suffix	-an	**tulis** (write)	**tulisan** (writing)
Confix	ke-...-an	**datang** (arrive)	**kedatangan** (arrival)
	pe-...-an	**terbang** (fly)	**penerbangan** (flight)

Verb affixes are attached to base words to form verbs:

Type	Affix	Root word	Derived word
Prefix	ber-	**fungsi** (function)	**berfungsi** (to function)
	me-	**telepon** (phone)	**menelepon** (to call)
	di-	**pesan** (order)	**dipesan** (to be ordered)
Suffix	-kan	**tunjuk** (show)	**tunjukkan** (to show)
	-i	**seberang** (across)	**seberangi** (to cross)
Confix	me-...-kan	**uang** (money)	**menguangkan** (to cash (a check))
	me-...-i	**teman** (companion)	**menemani** (to accompany)
	di-...-i	**kurang** (less)	**dikurangi** (to be reduced)
	di-...-kan	**lapor** (report)	**dilaporkan** (to be reported)

Adjective affixes are attached to base words to form adjectives:

Type	Affix	Root word	Derived word
Prefix	ter-	**buka** (open)	**terbuka** (ajar)

Nouns

Plural nouns can be formed by repeating the noun, or adding a qualifier. Repetition is only necessary if the plural meaning is not implied by the sentence. Example:

book **buku**
my books **buku-buku saya**
two books **dua buku**

Verbs

Indonesian verbs do not have singular or plural forms or present, past or future tenses. Time is expressed using adverbs of time such as yesterday, today, tomorrow, etc.

Negation

There are four forms of negation in Indonesian:

I'm not hungry. **Saya tidak lapar.** (for verbs and adjectives)

He's not a tourist. **Dia bukan turis.** (for nouns)

She has not given me the change yet. **Dia belum memberi saya kembalian.**

Do not eat too much. **Jangan makan terlalu banyak.** (imperative)

Questions

Questions are formed using question words which work very much like their English counterparts.

who **siapa**

what **apa**

when **kapan**

which **yang mana**

where **di mana**

how **bagaimana**

how much **berapa**

Examples:

Who are you? **Siapa anda?**

What is this? **Apa ini?**

Questions can also be formed by adding the word **apakah** in front of the sentence:

Ini aman This is safe.

Apakah ini aman? Is this safe?

Adjectives

Adjectives are placed after nouns in Indonesian:

car **mobil**

red car **mobil merah**

Adverbs

Adverbs in Indonesian are usually preceded by **dengan** or **secara**. They appear after the verbs they modify:

quick **cepat**

quickly **secara cepat**

runs quickly **berlari secara cepat**

Measure Words

Indonesian uses measure words, which are combined with numerals, to count nouns. The most three common measure words are **orang** (for people), **ekor** (for animals), and **buah** (for non-living things). When there is only one object, the numeral prefix **se-** is used in front of the measure word, not **satu**.

two waiters **dua orang pelayan**

three birds **tiga ekor burung**

one car **sebuah mobil**

In spoken language, it is common for people to just use the numeral and the noun, and drop the measure word.

Prepositions

The most common prepositions are **di**, **ke**, and **dari**.

Examples:

I'm at the train station **Saya berada di stasiun kereta.**

I moved from Jakarta to Bandung **Saya pindah dari Jakarta ke Bandung.**

Numbers

ESSENTIAL

0	**nol**	*nol*
1	**satu**	*sah·too*
2	**dua**	*doo·wah*
3	**tiga**	*tee·gah*
4	**empat**	*əm·paht*
5	**lima**	*lee·mah*
6	**enam**	*ə·nahm*
7	**tujuh**	*too·jooh*
8	**delapan**	*də·lah·pahn*
9	**sembilan**	*səm·bee·lahn*
10	**sepuluh**	*sə·poo·looh*
11	**sebelas**	*sə·bə·lahs*
12	**dua belas**	*doo·wah bə·lahs*
13	**tiga belas**	*tee·gah bə·lahs*
14	**empat belas**	*əm·paht bə·lahs*
15	**lima belas**	*lee·mah bə·lahs*
16	**enam belas**	*ə·nahm bə·lahs*
17	**tujuh belas**	*too·jooh bə·lahs*
18	**delapan belas**	*də·lah·pahn bə·lahs*
19	**sembilan belas**	*səm·bee·lahn bə·lahs*
20	**dua puluh**	*doo·wah poo·looh*
21	**dua puluh satu**	*doo·wah poo·looh sah·too*
22	**dua puluh dua**	*doo·wah poo·looh doo·wah*
30	**tiga puluh**	*tee·gah poo·looh*
31	**tiga puluh satu**	*tee·gah poo·looh sah·too*
40	**empat puluh**	*əm·paht poo·looh*
50	**lima puluh**	*lee·mah poo·looh*

60	**enam puluh** ə·nahm poo·looh
70	**tujuh puluh** too·jooh poo·looh
80	**delapan puluh** də·lah·pahn poo·looh
90	**sembilan puluh** səm·bee·lahn poo·looh
100	**seratus** sə·rah·toos
101	**seratus satu** sə·rah·toos sah·too
200	**dua ratus** doo·wah rah·toos
500	**lima ratus** lee·mah rah·toos
1,000	**seribu** sə·ree·boo
10,000	**sepuluh ribu** sə·poo·looh ree·boo
100,000	**seratus ribu** sə·rah·toos ree·boo
1,000,000	**satu juta** sə·joo·tah

Ordinal Numbers

first	**pertama** pər·tah·mah
second	**kedua** kə·doo·wah
third	**ketiga** kə·tee·gah
fourth	**keempat** kə·əm·paht
fifth	**kelima** kə·lee·mah
once	**sekali** sə·kah·lee
twice	**dua kali** doo·wah kah·lee
three times	**tiga kali** tee·gah kah·lee

Time

ESSENTIAL

What time is it?	**Jam berapa sekarang?** *jahm bə·rah·pah sə·kah·rahng*
It's noon [midday].	**Sekarang tengah hari.** *sə·kah·rahng tə·ngah hah·ree*
At midnight.	**Pada tengah malam.** *pah·dah tə·ngah mah·lahm*
From one o'clock to two o'clock.	**Dari jam satu hingga jam dua.** *dah·ree jahm sah·too hing·gah jahm doo·wah*
Five after [past] three.	**Jam tiga lebih lima.** *jahm tee·gah lə·beeh lee·mah*
A quarter to four.	**Jam empat kurang seperempat** *jahm əm·paht koo·rahng sə·pər·em·paht*
5:30 a.m./p.m.	**5:30 pagi/sore.** *5:30 pah·gee/soh·reh*

Days

ESSENTIAL

Monday	**Senin** *sə·nin*
Tuesday	**Selasa** *sə·lah·sah*
Wednesday	**Rabu** *rah·boo*
Thursday	**Kamis** *kah·miss*
Friday	**Jumat** *joom·aht*
Saturday	**Sabtu** *sahb·too*
Sunday	**Minggu** *ming·goo*

Dates

Reference

yesterday	**kemarin** *kə·mah·rin*
today	**hari ini** *hah·ree ee·nee*
tomorrow	**besok** *beh·sok*
day	**hari** *hah·ree*
week	**minggu** *ming·goo*
month	**bulan** *boo·lahn*
year	**tahun** *tah·hoon*

Months

January	**Januari** *jah·noo·wah·ree*
February	**Februari** *feh·broo·wah·ree*
March	**Maret** *mah·rət*
April	**April** *ah·pril*
May	**Mei** *may*
June	**Juni** *joo·nee*
July	**Juli** *joo·lee*
August	**Agustus** *ah·goos·toos*
September	**September** *sep·tem·bər*
October	**Oktober** *ok·to·bər*
November	**November** *no·vem·bər*
December	**Desember** *deh·sem·bər*

Seasons

in/during the…	**dalam/selama…** *dah·lahm/sə·lah·mah*
spring	**musim semi** *moo·sim sə·mee*
summer	**musim panas** *moo·sim pah·nahs*
fall [autumn]	**musim gugur** *moo·sim goo·goor*
winter	**musim dingin** *moo·sim dee·ngin*

Holidays

New Year's Day (Jan 1)

Chinese New Year (based on the Chinese Lunar calendar, the first day of the first Lunar month)

Awal Muharram
(also known as **Maal Hijrah**, based on the Islamic calendar)

Day of Silence
(also known as **Hari Raya Nyepi**, based on Balinese calendar)

Prophet Muhammad's Birthday
(also known as **Maulidur Rasul**, based on the Islamic calendar)

Good Friday (date varies yearly)

Ascension Day (May 1) (falls 40 days after Easter Sunday)

Wesak Day (based on the Chinese Lunar calendar)

Isra & Mi'raj
(also known as **Lailat al Miraj**, based on the Islamic calendar)

Independence Day (Aug 17)

Hari Raya Puasa
(also known as **Eid-ul-Fitri**, based on the Islamic calendar)

Hari Raya Haji
(also known as **Eid-ul-Adha**, Muslims will usually make their pilgrimage to Mecca at this time)

Christmas Day (Dec 25)

The actual dates of some holidays vary annually according to local customs and respective calendars, such as the Chinese lunar calendar, Islamic calendar and Balinese calendar. Apart from the above, nine joint holidays (**cuti bersama**) are declared nationwide by the Indonesian government at various times of the year.

Conversion Tables

When you know	Multiply by	To find
ounces	28.3	grams
pounds	0.45	kilograms
inches	2.54	centimeters
feet	0.3	meters
miles	1.61	kilometers
square inches	6.45	sq. centimeters
square feet	0.09	sq. meters
square miles	2.59	sq. kilometers
pints (US/Brit)	0.47/0.56	liters
gallons (US/Brit)	3.8/4.5	liters
Fahrenheit	5/9, after −32	Centigrade
Centigrade	9/5, then +32	Fahrenheit

Kilometers to Miles Conversions

1 km – 0.62 mi	20 km – 12.4 mi
5 km – 3.1 mi	50 km – 31 mi
10 km – 6.2 mi	100 km – 61 mi

Measurement

1 gram	= 0.035 oz.
1 kilogram (kg)	= 2.2 lb
1 liter (l)	= 1.06 U.S/0.88 Brit. quarts
1 centimeter (cm)	= 0.4 inch
1 meter (m)	= 3.28 feet
1 kilometer (km)	= 0.62 mile

Temperature

-40° C – -40° F	-1° C – 30° F	20° C – 68° F
-30° C – -22° F	0° C – 32° F	25° C – 77° F
-20° C – -4° F	5° C – 41° F	30° C – 86° F
-10° C – 14° F	10° C – 50° F	
-5° C – 23° F	15° C – 59° F	

Oven Temperature

100° C – 212° F	177° C – 350° F
121° C – 250° F	204° C – 400° F
149° C – 300° F	260° C – 500° F

Dictionary

as kamera
toko kamera
.emah
ove tungku untuk

perkemahan
(yes) kaleng; bisa / dapat
ener pembuka kaleng
ian (person) Orang Kanada
el v membatalkan
y permen
ds makanan kaleng

Celsius Celsius
centimeter centimeter
ceramic spoon sendok
cereal cereal
certificate sertifikat
chair lift (cable c
chair kursi
change v
change
cha
c

English–Indonesian

A

a.m. pagi
accept *v* menerima
access akses
accident kecelakaan
accommodation akomodasi
account *n* rekening
adapter adaptor
address *n* alamat
admission (fees) tiket masuk
after setelah / sesudah
afternoon siang
aftershave aftershave
again lagi
age umur / usia
agency agen
AIDS AIDS
air udara
air conditioning AC
airline penerbangan
airmail pos udara
airplane pesawat terbang
airport bandara
airport tax pajak bandara
aisle seat tempat duduk di pinggir
aisle lorong
alarm clock jam alarm

alcohol alkohol
allergic reaction suka alergi
allergic alergi
allow *v* membolehkan
alone sendirian
alter *v* **(clothing)** ganti
alternate route rute alternatif
aluminum foil kertas timah aluminium
amazing mengagumkan
ambulance ambulan
American Amerika
amount jumlah
amusement park taman hiburan
anemic anemia
anesthesia *n* anestesi
animal hewan
ankle tumit
antibiotic antibiotik
antiques store toko barang antik
antiseptic antiseptik
anyone siapa saja
anything apa saja / sesuatu
apartment apartemen
appendix (body part) usus buntu
appetizer hidangan pembuka
apple apel
appointment perjanjian *n* /

adj adjective	**BE** British English	**prep** preposition
adv adverb	**n** noun	**v** verb

buat janji v
apricot aprikot
arcade arena bermain
area code kode area
arm lengan
around (the corner) di balik tikungan
arrivals (airport) kedatangan
arrive v datang / tiba
artery arteri / nadi
arthritis peradangan sendi
artificial artifisial / buatan
Asian (restaurant) Asia
asparagus asparagus
aspirin aspirin
assistance bantuan
asthma asthma
ATM card kartu ATM
attached (in a relationship) sudah
    punya pacar
attack (on person) menyerang
attend v hadir
attraction (place) tempat menarik
attractive menarik
audio audio / suara
Australian (person) Orang Australia
authentic asli
automatic car mobil otomatis

B

baby bottle botol bayi
baby food makanan bayi
baby wipe penyeka untuk bayi
baby bayi
babysitter penjaga bayi

back (body part) punggung
backpack ransel
bacon bacon
bag tas
baggage bagasi
baggage claim ambil koper / ambil
    bagasi
baggage ticket tiket bagasi
bake v memanggang
bakery toko roti-kue
ballet balet
bikini bikini
bill v **(charge)** biaya
bill n **(money)** bon / kwitansi
bird burung
birthday ulang tahun
bites n gigitan
black pepper merica hitam
black hitam
bladder kantung kemih
bland hambar
blanket selimut
bleed v berdarah
blood pressure tekanan darah
blood darah
blouse blus
blow-dry (hair) blow-dry
blue biru
board v menaiki
boarding pass tiket masuk pesawat
boat kapal
boil (cooking method) rebus
bone tulang
book n; v buku n; memesan v

bookstore toko buku

boots sepatu bot

boring membosankan

botanical garden kebun raya

bother v menganggu

bottle opener pembuka botol

bottle botol

bowl mangkuk

box boks / kotak

boxing match pertandingan tinju

boy anak laki

boyfriend pacar

bra BH

bracelet gelang

brakes (car) rem

brave adj berani

bread roti

breaded (cooking method) dibalut tepung roti

break v istirahat

break down v rusak

breakfast sarapan / makan pagi

break-in (burglary) maling

breast dada

breastfeed menyusui

breathe deeply tarik nafas panjang

breathe v bernafas

bridge jembatan

briefs (clothing) celana dalam

bring v membawa

British Inggris

broccoli brokoli

broken (bone) patah

broken (machine) rusak

broken (glass) pecah

brooch bros

broom sapu

brother (older) kakak

brother (younger) adik

brown cokelat

bug kecoa

building gedung

burn v membakar

bus station stasiun bis

bus stop terminal bis

bus ticket tiket bis

bus tour tur dengan bis

bus bis

business bisnis / usaha

business center pusat bisnis

business class kelas bisnis

business hours jam buka

banana pisang

bandage perban

bank bank

bar (place) bar

barbecue memanggang

barber tempat cukur

baseball bisbol

basket (grocery store) keranjang

basketball basket

bathroom kamar mandi

batik batik

battery baterai

battleground medan perang

be v menjadi

beach pantai

bean curd tahu

beautiful indah / cantik
bed and breakfast tempat tidur dan sarapan
bed tempat tidur
beef sapi
beer bir
before sebelum
begin v mulai
beginner (skill level) pemula
behind (direction) di belakang
beige gading tua
belt ikat pinggang
berth (on boat / train) tempat tidur
best terbaik
bet v bertaruh
better lebih baik
beverage minuman
bicycle sepeda
big besar
bigger lebih besar
bike route rute sepeda
busy sibuk
butcher tukang daging
butter mentega
buttocks bokong
buy v membeli
bye bye

C

cabbage kol
cabin kabin
cable car kereta gantung
café kafe
call v memanggil

calories kalori
camera kamera
camera case tas kamera
camera store toko kamera
camp v berkemah
camping stove tungku untuk berkemah
campsite perkemahan
can n; v **(yes)** kaleng; bisa / dapat
can opener pembuka kaleng
Canadian (person) Orang Kanada
cancel v membatalkan
candy permen
canned goods makanan kaleng
canyon ngarai
capsicum paprika
car hire [BE] sewa mobil
car park [BE] pelataran parkir mobil
car rental penyewaan mobil
car seat tempat duduk di mobil
car mobil
carafe karafe
carambola [starfruit] belimbing
card kartu
carp (fish) kerapu
carrot wortel
carry-on jinjingan / dijinjing
cart kereta
carton karton
carvings n ukiran
cash v uang / tunai
cash advance uang muka
cashier kasir
casino kasino

castle kastil
cathedral kathedral
Catholic Katolik
cauliflower kembang kol
cave gua
CD CD
celery seledri
cell phone ponsel
telefon telepon
Celsius Celsius
centimeter centimeter
ceramic spoon sendok keramik
cereal cereal
certificate sertifikat
chair lift (cable car) kursi gantung
chair kursi
change v mengubah
change n **(money)** kembalian
charcoal arang
charge v **(credit card)** menagih
cheap murah
cheaper lebih murah
check v **(something)** memeriksa
check n cek
check-in check-in
check-out check-out
checking account rekening giro
cheese keju
chemical toilet toilet kimia
chemist [BE] apotek
cheque [BE] cek
cherry ceri
chest (body part) dada
chest pain sakit dada

chewing gum permen karet
chicken ayam
child anak
child's seat tempat duduk anak
children's portion porsi anak
China China
Chinese (person) Orang China
chocolates cokelat
chopsticks sumpit
church gereja
cigar cerutu
cigarette rokok
city hall balai kota
clam kerang
class kelas
classical music musik klasik
clay pot periuk tembikar
clean v; **clean** adj membersihkan v;
    bersih adj
cleaning product produk pembersih
cleaning supplies perlengkapan
    pembersih
clear v membersihkan
cliff jurang
clock jam
close v; **close** adj tutup v; dekat adj
closed tutup
clothing pakaian
clothing store toko pakaian
club klub
coat jas
cod (type of fish) cod
coffee shop coffee shop
coin koin

cola kola
cold dingin
cold (sickness) flu
colleague kolega / rekan
collect call panggilan collect
cologne minyak wangi
color warna
comb sisir
come *v* datang
company (firm) perusahaan
complain mengeluh
complaint keluhan
computer komputer
concert hall aula konser
concert konser
condition (medical) kondisi
conditioner (hair) conditioner
condom kondom
conference konferensi
confirm *v* konfirm
congestion kepadatan
connect *v* (internet) sambung
connection (internet) koneksi / sambungan
constipated sembelit
consulate konsulat
consultant konsultan
contact *v* kontak
contact lens lensa kontak
contagious menular
contain berisi
convention hall aula konvensi
conversion table tabel konversi
conveyor belt ban berjalan / konveyor

cook *v* memasak
cooking gas LPG
cool (temperature) sejuk
copper tembaga
corkscrew pencungkil tutup gabus
corn (vegetable) jagung
corner sudut
cost biaya / harga
costume kostum
cot buaian / tempat tidur bayi
cotton katun
cough batuk
counter *n* gerai / counter
country code kode negara
court (sports) lapangan
cover charge cover charge
crab (animal) kepiting
cramps (menstruation) kejang
crash *v* (car) tabrakan
cream / ointment krim / minyak gosok
credit card kartu kredit
crew neck lingkar leher baju
crib tempat tidur bayi
crystal kristal
cup cangkir
cured meat daging asin
currency mata uang
currency exchange kurs mata uang
currency exchange office kantor penukaran mata uang asing
current account *[BE]* rekening koran
customs pabean / bea-cukai
cut *v* (hair); **cut** *n* (injury) memangkas *v*; luka *n*

cute mungil
cycling bersepeda

D

dairy produk susu
damage v; **damage n** merusak v; kerusakan n
damaged rusak
dance club klub dansa
dance v dansa / menari
dancing berdansa / tarian
danger bahaya
dark gelap
date (calendar) tanggal
dates (fruit) kurma
day hari
deaf tuli
debit card kartu debit
decision keputusan
deck chair kursi pantai
declare v menyatakan
decline v **(credit card)** menolak
deeply mendalam
degrees (temperature) derajat
delay v; **delay n** menunda v; tunda n
delete v menghapus
delicatessen toko daging olah
delicious enak / lezat
denim denim
dentist dokter gigi
denture gigi palsu
deodorant deodorant
department store pusat pertokoan
departure keberangkatan

deposit v; **deposit** n **(bank)** menyetor v; deposito n
detergent deterjen
diabetes diabetes
dial v memutar
diamond intan
diaper popok
diarrhea diare
diesel solar
difficult sulit
digital photo foto digital
digital print cetak foto digital
dining room ruang makan
dinner makan malam
direction arah
dirty kotor
disabled accessible [BE] dapat dilalui penyandang cacat
disabled cacat
disconnect (computer) putuskan hubungan
discount diskon
dish (kitchen) piring
dishes (food) masakan
dishwasher mesin cuci piring
dishwashing liquid sabun cair pencuci piring
display case lemari pajangan
display v; **display n** memajang v; pajangan n
disposable razor silet cukur sekali pakai
disposable sekali pakai
dive v menyelam

diving equipment perlengkapan menyelam

divorce v; **divorce** n bercerai v; perceraian n

dizzy pusing

do not disturb jangan diganggu

doctor dokter

dog anjing

doll boneka

dollar (U.S.) dolar

domestic flight penerbangan domestik

domestic domestik

door pintu

dormitory asrama

double bed tempat tidur untuk berdua

downtown pusat kota

dozen lusin

draw menggambar

drawer laci

dress (piece of clothing) baju

dress code aturan busana

drink menu menu minuman

drink v; **drink** n minum v; minuman n

drinking water air minum

drive v mengemudi

driver's license number nomor sim pengemudi

drop (medicine) obat tetes

drowsiness pusing / pening

dry cleaner dry cleaner

duck (animal) bebek

during sewaktu / selama

duty (tax) cukai

duty-free bebas pajak

DVD DVD

E

ear telinga

earache sakit telinga

early awal

earrings anting

east timur

easy mudah

eat v makan

economy class kelas ekonomi

egg telur

eggplant [aubergine] terong

elbow siku

electric outlet soket listrik

elevator lift

e-mail address alamat e-mail

e-mail e-mail

emergency exit pintu darurat

emergency darurat

empty; empty v kosong; mengosongkan

end v mengakhiri

engaged (in a relationship) bertunangan

English bahasa Inggris

engrave v mengukir

enjoy v menikmati

enter v memasuki

entertainment hiburan

entrance jalan masuk

envelope amplop

epilepsy ayan / epilepsi

equipment perlengkapan

escalator eskalator / tangga berjalan

e-ticket e-ticket

evening malam

excess ekses

exchange rate kurs

exchange v menukar

excursion darmawisata

excuse me v maaf / permisi

excuse n alasan

exhausted lelah

exit v; **exit** n keluar v; pengeluaran n

expensive mahal mahal

expert (skill level) ahli

expiration date tanggal kedaluwarsa

express kilat / ekspres

extension (phone) nomor pesawat

external use penggunaan eksternal

extra large (size) ekstra besar

extra small (size) ekstra kecil

extra ekstra

extract v **(tooth)** mencabut

eye mata

F

fabric kain / bahan

face wajah

facial facial

facility fasilitas

family keluarga

fan (appliance) kipas

far jauh

fare (e.g taxi fare) ongkos

farm pertanian / perkebunan

far-sighted (eye condition) rabun jauh

fast food makanan cepat saji

fast cepat

faster lebih cepat

fat free bebas lemak

father ayah / bapak

fax number nomor faks

fax v; **fax** n memfaks v; faks n

fee biaya

feed v memberi makan

ferry feri

fever demam

field (sports) lapangan

fill out v **(form)** mengisi

fill up v **(food)** menambah

filling (tooth) menambal

film (camera) film

fine (fee) denda

fine (greetings) baik

finger jari

fingernail kuku jari

fire kebakaran / api

fire department pemadam kebakaran

fire door pintu darurat

first pertama

first class kelas satu

fit (clothing) pas

fitting room ruang pas

fix v **(repair)** perbaiki

fixed-price menu menu harga pasti

flashlight senter

flats (shoes) datar

flight penerbangan

floor lantai
florist toko bunga
flower bunga
fly v terbang
fly (insect) lalat
folk music musik rakyat
food makanan
foot kaki
football game [BE] sepakbola
for untuk
forecast ramalan
forest hutan
fork garpu
form (fill-in) formulir
formula (baby) formula
fountain air mancur
free gratis / bebas
freezer freezer
fresh segar
fried (cooking method) digoreng
friend teman
fruits buah-buahan
frying pan penggorengan
full penuh
full-service layanan lengkap
fun asyik
funny lucu / kocak

G

game permainan
garage garasi
garbage bag kantung sampah
garlic bawang putih
gas station pompa bensin

gas gas
gate (airport) gerbang
gay (happy) senang
gel (hair) gel
get off (a train / bus / subway) turun
get to pergi ke
gift hadiah
gin gin
girl putri / anak perempuan
girlfriend teman perempuan
give v memberi
glass (drinking) gelas
glass (material) kaca
glasses (spectacles) kacamata
gluten ketan
go v **(somewhere)** pergi
gold emas
golf course lapangan golf
golf tournament turnamen golf
good bagus / baik
good afternoon selamat siang
good evening selamat malam
good morning selamat pagi
goodbye selamat tinggal
goods barang
grandchild cucu
grandchildren cucu-cucu
grandfather kakek
grandmother nenek
grape anggur
grapefruit jeruk keprok
grater parutan
gray abu-abu
green hijau

grocery store toko bahan makanan
ground floor lantai dasar
group grup / kelompok
guide (tourist) *n* pemandu
guide book buku panduan
guide dog anjing pemandu
gym gym
gynecologist dokter kandungan

H

hair dryer pengering rambut
hair salon salon rambut
hair rambut
hairbrush sikat rambut
haircut gunting rambut
hairspray hairspray
hairstyle tata rambut
hairstylist penata rambut
halal halal
half hour setengah jam
half setengah / separuh
half-kilo setengah kilo
hall aula
ham (food) ham
hammer palu
hand luggage *[BE]* kopor tangan
hand tangan
handbag *[BE]* tas tangan
handicapped cacat
handicapped-accessible dapat dilalui
    penyandang cacat
hangover teler
happy senang
hat topi

have *v* mempunyai / memiliki
hawker centre pusat kaki lima
hay fever alergi akibat tanaman
headache sakit kepala
headphones headphone
health food store toko makanan
    kesehatan
health kesehatan
hearing impaired gangguan
    pendengaran
heart condition sakit jantung
heart hati / jantung
heat panas
heater alat pemanas
heating *[BE]* pemanasan
height tinggi
hello halo
helmet helm
help bantuan
here di sini
hi hai
high tinggi
highchair kursi tinggi
high-heels hak sepatu tinggi
highlights (hair) highlight
highway jalan bebas hambatan
hill bukit
hire *v [BE]* sewa
hired car *[BE]* mobil sewa
hitchhike *v* menumpang
hockey hoki
hold *v* pegang / tahan
holiday *[BE]* liburan
home rumah

hospital rumah sakit
hostel hostel
hot (temperature); hot (spicy) panas; pedas
hot water air panas
hotel hotel
hour jam
house rumah
household goods perabotan rumah
housekeeping services layanan housekeeping
how are you apa kabar
how much (price) berapa harganya
how bagaimana
hug v peluk
hungry lapar
hurt sakit
husband suami

I

I Saya
ibuprofen (see painkiller) ibuprofen
ice es
icy mengandung es
identification (card) identifikasi
ill sakit
immigration imigrasi
in di
include v termasuk
indoor di dalam ruangan
indoor pool kolam renang dalam ruangan
inexpensive tidak mahal
infected terinfeksi

infection infeksi
information informasi
information desk meja informasi
insect bite gigitan serangga
insect repellent pengusir serangga
insert v (on an ATM) masukkan
inside di dalam
insomnia sulit tidur
instant message pesan instan
insulin insulin
insurance asuransi
insurance company perusahaan asuransi
interested tertarik
interesting menarik
international internasional
international flight penerbangan internasional
international student pelajar internasional
internet internet
internet cafe kafe internet
internet service layanan internet
interpreter penerjemah lisan
intersection persimpangan
into ke dalam
introduce v memperkenalkan
invoice faktur
Irish (person) orang Irlandia
iron (clothes) v; **Iron** n setrika v; besi n
itemize daftar barang

J

jacket jaket

jackfruit nangka
jade batu giok
jam (food) selai
jam (traffic) *v;* **jam** macet (traffic) *v;*
   menghambat
jar toples
jaw rahang
jazz club klub jazz
jazz jazz
jeans jeans
jelly (food) jeli
jeweler toko perhiasan
jewelry perhiasan
join *v* gabung
joint (body part) persendian
joke gurauan
juice jus

K

keep simpan
keep refrigerated simpan di
   lemari es
key; key card kunci; kartu kunci
key ring gantungan kunci
kick tendang
kiddie pool kolam renang anak
kidney (body part) ginjal
kilogram kilogram
kilometer kilometer
kind (person) baik
kiss *v* cium
kitchen dapur
kiwi fruit kiwi
knee lutut

knife pisau
know tahu
knowledge pengetahuan

L

lactose intolerant tidak tahan gula
lady wanita / perempuan
lake danau
lamb (meat) kambing
lamp lampu
language bahasa
large besar
last terakhir
last night tadi malam
last week minggu lalu
late (time) terlambat
later nanti
laundromat laundromat / mesin cuci
   otomatis
laundry laundry
laundry facility fasilitas laundry
laundry service servis laundry
lawyer pengacara
lazy malas
leaded (fuel) timbal
leaf daun
learn, *v* belajar
leather kulit
leave (depart) *v* **(planes); leave
   (buses, trains, etc.)** berangkat *v*
left (direction) kiri
leg kaki
lemon lemon
lemonade air jeruk

lemongrass sereh
lens lensa
less kurang
lesson (learnt a lesson) pelajaran
letter surat
lettuce selada
library perpustakaan
licence lisensi / surat izin
life boat perahu penyelamat
life jacket jaket pelampung
lifeguard penjaga
lift lift
light v; **light** v **(cigarette)** api v;
  menyalakan rokok v
light adj **(bright); light** adj **(not
  heavy)** terang adj; ringan adj
lightbulb bohlam
lighter pemantik rokok (cigarette) /
  lebih ringan (less heavy)
like v menyukai
lime jeruk nipis
line jalur
lip bibir
liquor store toko minuman keras
liter liter
little kecil
live v mendiami / tinggal
liver (body part) hati
loafers sendal
lobster lobster
local lokal
lock n kunci
lock up mengunci
locker lemari

log off mematikan
log on menyambung
long sleeves lengan panjang
long panjang
long-sighted [BE] rabun-jauh
look v melihat
lose v **(something)** kehilangan
lost and found tempat pengaduan
  barang hilang
lost hilang
lotion lotion
loud keras / nyaring
love cinta
low rendah
luggage kopor
luggage cart kereta koper / troli
luggage locker lemari kopor
lunch makan siang
lung paru-paru

M

magazine majalah
Madam / Mrs Ibu / Nyonya
magnificent luar biasa
mail v; **mail** n menyurati v; surat n
mailbox kotak surat
main attraction tempat utama yang
  menarik
main course hidangan utama
make up (face) v rias / make up
mall mal
man pria
manager manajer
mango mangga

manicure manikur
manual car mobil manual
map *n* peta
market pasar
married menikah
marry *v* menikah
mass (church service) misa
massage pijat
mat (rug) tikar
match n pertandingan
meal makan
measure *v* **(someone)** mengukur
measuring cup gelas takaran
measuring spoon sendok takaran
mechanic mekanis
medicine obat
medium (size) medium
meet *v* **(someone)** menemui / bertemu
meeting room ruang rapat
meeting pertemuan / rapat
membership card kartu keanggotaan
memorial (place) memorial
memory card kartu memori
mend *v* memperbaiki
men's milik pria
menstrual cramp kejang kalau haid
menstruation haid
menu menu
message pesan
meter (parking) meteran parkir
microwave ketuhar microwave
midday *[BE]* tengah hari
midnight tengah malam
mileage mil

milk susu
mini-bar mini-bar
minute menit
Miss Saudari / Nona
missing (something); missing (someone) kehilangan; rindu / kangen
mistake kesalahan / salah
mobile phone *[BE]* ponsel
mobility mobilitas
money uang
monorail monorail
month bulan
mop alat pel
more lagi
morning pagi
mosque mesjid
mother ibu
motion sickness mabuk karena goyangan
motor boat perahu motor
motorcycle sepeda motor
motorway (highway) *[BE]* jalan raya (highway)
mountain gunung
mousse (hair) mousse
mouth mulut
movie theater bioskop
movie film
Mr / Sir Saudara / Tuan / Bapak
Mrs / Madam Nyonya / Ibu
mug *v* cangkir
multiple-trip (ticket) tiket pulang-pergi

muscle otot
museum museum
mushroom jamur
music store toko musik
music musik

N

nail kuku
name nama
napkin serbet
nappy *[BE]* popok
nationality kebangsaan
nature preserve cagar alam
nauseous mual
near; nearby dekat; di sekitar
near-sighted rabun dekat
neck; necklace leher; kalung
need *v* memerlukan
new baru
newspaper surat kabar / koran
newsstand kios koran
next to di samping
next berikutnya / di samping
nice menyenangkan
night malam
nightclub klub malam
no tidak
non-alcoholic tanpa alkohol
non-smoking tidak merokok
noodles mie
noon tengah hari
north utara
nose hidung
notes *[BE]* catatan

nothing tidak ada apa-apa
notify *v* memberitahu
novice (skill level) pemula
now sekarang
number nomor
nurse perawat
nuts (food) kacang

O

office kantor
oatmeal oatmeal
octopus gurita
office hours jam kerja
oil oli / minyak
OK OK
old (person); old (long ago) tua; lama
old town kota tua
olive zaitun
on the corner di sudut / di tikungan
once sekali
one satu
one-way (ticket) sekali jalan
one-way street jalan satu arah
only hanya
on-time tepat waktu
open buka
opera opera
opposite di seberang
optician ahli mata
orange (color) oranye / jingga
orchestra orkestra
order *v* memesan
outdoor pool kolam di luar ruangan
outside di luar

over the counter (medication) beli bebas
overdone terlalu matang
overnight semalaman
ox sapi jantan
oxtail buntut sapi
oyster tiram

P

p.m. siang / sore
pacifier dot bayi
pack v membereskan / mengepak
package kemasan / paket
pad (for menstruation) pembalut wanita
paddling pool [BE] kolam renang anak
pages (in a book) halaman
pain kesakitan
painkiller obat penghilang sakit
pajamas piyama
palace istana
pants celana panjang
pantyhose pantyhose
papaya (fruit) pepaya
paper towel handuk kertas
paper kertas
paracetamol [BE] (see painkiller) paracetamol
park v; **park** n parkir v; taman n
parking lot pelataran parkir
parking meter meteran parkir
part-time paruh waktu
passenger penumpang
passport control kontrol paspor

passport paspor
password kata sandi
pastry shop toko kue
path jalur
pay phone telepon bayar
pay v membayar
pea ercis
peach peach
peak (of a mountain) puncak
pear pir
pearl mutiara
pedestrian pejalan kaki
pediatrician dokter anak
pedicure pedikur
peeled (cooking method) dikupas
pen pena
penicillin penisilin
penis penis
pepper merica
per; per hour; per day; per night; per week per; per jam; per hari; per malam; per minggu
perfume parfum
period (menstrual) haid
period (of time) jangka waktu / periode
permissible according to Islamic law diizinkan menurut hukum Islam
permit v mengizinkan
personal identification number (PIN) nomor identifikasi pribadi
petite mungil
petrol [BE] bensin
petrol station [BE] pompa bensin

pewter barang dari alpaka
pharmacy farmasi
phone v; **phone** n menelepon v;
  telepon n
phone call panggilan telepon
phone card kartu telepon
phone number nomor telepon
photo foto
photocopy fotokopi
photography fotografi
pick up (something) mengambil
picnic area area piknik
piece sepotong
pill (birth control) pil
pillow bantal
pineapple nanas
pink merah muda
pizzeria pizzeria
place n tempat
plan rencana
plane pesawat terbang
plastic plastik
plastic wrap bungkus plastik
plate piring
platform peron
platinum platinum
play v; **play** n (theatre) bermain v;
  sandiwara n
playground taman bermain
playpen playpen
please tolong, silakan, harap
pleased senang
plum plum
plunger penyedot wc

plus size ukuran plus
poach (cooking method) dimasak
  tanpa kulit
pocket saku
poison racun
police polisi
police report laporan polisi
police station kantor polisi
pomegranate delima
pomelo jeruk bali
pond kolam
pool kolam renang
pop music musik pop
porcelain porselen
pork babi
porridge bubur
portion porsi
post [BE] pos
post office kantor pos
postbox [BE] kotak pos
postcard kartu pos
pot periuk
potato kentang
pottery (goods) barang tembikar
poultry unggas
pregnant hamil
prescribe v menulis resep
prescription resep
press v (clothing) setrika
price harga
print v mencetak
problem masalah
prohibit v dilarang
pronounce v mengucapkan

Protestant Protestan
public publik
pull v tarik
purple ungu
purpose tujuan
purse tas kecil
push v dorong
pushchair kursi dorong

Q

quality kualitas
queen ratu
question pertanyaan
queue antre
quick cepat
quiet tenang

R

rabbit kelinci
radio radio
radish radis
railway station [BE] stasiun kereta api
rain n hujan
raincoat jas hujan
rainforest hutan tadah hujan
ramp ramp
rap (music) rap
rape perkosa
rare (object) jarang
rash n gatal-gatal
rate (exchange rate) kurs
rat tikus
ravine jurang / ngarai
raw mentah

reach v mencapai / menjangkau
read baca
ready siap
real asli / nyata
really sungguh
reason alasan
receipt resi / tanda terima
receive v menerima
recharge v mengisi ulang
recommend v merekomendasi
recommendation rekomendasi
recycling daur ulang
red merah
refrigerator lemari es
refund pengembalian dana
region wilayah
registered mail surat tercatat
regular (normal) biasa
relationship hubungan
rent v menyewa
rental car mobil sewa
repair v memperbaiki
repeat v mengulang
reservation desk meja reservasi
reservation reservasi
reserve v memesan tempat
resort (holiday) resor
restaurant restoran
restroom (formal / informal) kamar
  kecil / wc
retired pensiun
return (something) v
  (return ticket) n
  [BE] mengembalikan v

(tiket pulang-pergi) *n*
reverse *v* **(the charges)**
    [BE] membalikkan
rib (body part) rusuk
rice beras
right (direction) kanan
right of way sebelah kanan
ring cincin
river sungai
road jalan
road map peta jalan
roast *v* panggang
rob *v* merampok
robbed dirampok
romantic romantis
room kamar
room key kunci kamar
room service room service
round-trip perjalanan pulang-pergi
rotten busuk
rubbish *[BE]* sampah
rubbish bag *[BE]* kantung sampah
ruins puing / reruntuhan
run lari
rush (in a rush) terburu-buru

S

signature tanda tangan
sad sedih
safe (object); safe (protected) lemari
    besi; aman
sales tax pajak penjualan
salmon salmon
salon salon

salty asin
sandals sendal
sanitary napkin pembalut wanita
sauce saos
saucepan panci
sauna sauna
sausage sosis
sauteed (cooking method) ditumis
save *v* simpan
savings (account) tabungan
scallion [spring onion] daun bawang
scanner pemindai
schedule *n* jadwal
school sekolah
science ilmiah
scissors gunting
sea laut
seafood seafood
seat tempat duduk
seaweed rumput laut
security keamanan / sekuriti / satpam
see *v* lihat
self-service swalayan
sell *v* jual
send *v* kirim
senior citizen warga usia lanjut
separated (marriage) berpisah
service (in a restaurant) pelayanan
sexually transmitted
    disease penyakit yang ditularkan
    melalui hubungan seks
shampoo shampoo
sharp tajam
shaving cream krim cukur

sheet lembar / seprei
shellfish kerang
ship v **(mail)** kirim
shirt kemeja
shoe store toko sepatu
shoes sepatu
shop toko
shopping v belanja
shopping area pusat perbelanjaan
shopping centre [BE] pusat perbelanjaan
shopping mall mal perbelanjaan
short sleeves lengan pendek
short adj pendek / singkat
shorts celana pendek
short-sighted [BE] rabun-dekat
shoulder bahu
show v menunjukkan
shower (to wash) shower
shrimp udang
sick sakit
side dish hidangan pendamping
side effect efek samping
sightseeing tour tur darmawisata
sightseeing darmawisata
silk sutera
silver perak
single (unmarried) lajang / belum menikah
single bed tempat tidur untuk satu orang
single room kamar untuk satu orang
sink bak cuci
Sir / Mr Saudara / Tuan / Bapak

sister (elder); sister (younger) kakak perempuan (elder); adik perempuan
sit v duduk
size ukuran
skin kulit
skirt rok
sleep v tidur
sleeping bag kantung tidur
slice (of something) seiris
slippers selop
slower lebih lamban
slowly perlahan-lahan
small kecil
smaller lebih kecil
smoke v merokok
smoking area area untuk merokok
snack bar snack bar
snacks cemilan
sneaker sepatu kanvas
snorkeling equipment perlengkapan snorkeling
snow n salju
soap sabun
soccer sepak bola
sock kaus kaki
soda soda
some beberapa
soother [BE] dot bayi
sore throat sakit tenggorokan
sorry maaf
soup sup
sour asam
south selatan
souvenir store toko suvenir /

cenderamata
souvenir suvenir / cenderamata
soy bean kedelai
soymilk susu kedelai
spa spa
spare ribs tulang iga
sparkling water air bersoda
speak *v* bicara
special khusus
specialist (doctor) spesialis
specimen contoh
speeding mengebut / mengemudi
dengan kecepatan tinggi
spell *v* mengeja
spicy pedas / berbumbu
spinach bayam
spine (body part) tulang belakang
spoon sendok
sporting goods perlengkapan olahraga
sports massage pijat olahraga
sports olahraga
sprain *v* terkilir
squid cumi
stadium stadium
stairs tangga
stamp *v* (a ticket); **stamp** *n*
(postage) cap *v*; perangko *n*
start *v* mulai
starter *[BE]* starter
station stasiun
statue patung
stay *v* tinggal
steak steak
steal *v* mencuri

steam *n* uap
steamed (cooking method) dikukus
steamer pengukus
steep terjal
sterling silver perak murni
sting *n* sengatan
stolen dicuri
stomach perut
stomachache sakit perut
stop *v* stop / berhenti
store directory direktori toko
storey *[BE]* tingkat / loteng
stove kompor gas
straight ahead lurus
straight lurus
strange aneh
strawberry stroberi
stream (school) jurusan
stream kali / sungai kecil
stroller pejalan kaki
student pelajar
study *v* studi / belajar
stunning mencengangkan
style (hair) tata rambut
subtitle teks film
subway station stasiun subway
subway subway
sugar gula
suit jas
suitcase tas pakaian
sun matahari
sunblock tabir surya
sunburn sengatan matahari
sunglasses kacamata hitam

sunny cerah
sunstroke sengatan matahari
supermarket supermarket / swalayan
supervision supervisi / pengawasan
surfboard papan seluncur
swallow *v* menelan
sweater sweater
sweet (taste) manis
sweets *[BE]* permen
swelling membengkak
swim *v* berenang
swimsuit baju renang
swordfish ikan cucut
symbol (keyboard) simbol
syrup sirop

T

table meja
tablet (medicine) tablet
take (something) *v* mengambil
take away (food) *[BE]* bungkus
take off *v* **(clothes)** menanggalkan
tampon tampon
taste *v* mencicip
taxi taksi
tea teh
team tim
teaspoon sendok teh
telephone telepon
temperature suhu
temple (religious) puri / candi
temporary sementara
tennis tenis
tent; tent peg; tent pole tenda; pasak

tenda; tiang tenda
terminal (airport) terminal
terrible buruk sekali
text *v* **(send a message)** teks
thank *v* terima kasih
thank you terima kasih
that itu
theater teater
theft pencurian
there di sana
thief pencuri
thigh paha
thirsty haus
this ini
thrash [rubbish] sampah
throat tenggorokan
thunderstorm angin badai
ticket; ticket office tiket; loket
tie (clothing) dasi
tight *adj* ketat
tights *[BE]* celana panjang ketat
time; time table *[BE]* waktu; jadwal
tire ban
tired lelah
tissue tisu
to go untuk dibawa
toasted bread roti panggang
tobacconist toko tembakau
today hari ini
toe; toe nail jari kaki; kuku jari kaki
toilet *[BE]* WC
toilet paper kertas WC
tomorrow besok
tongue lidah

tonight malam ini
too juga
tooth; tooth paste gigi; pasta gigi
top up card (phone value) kartu isi
total (amount) jumlah
tough (food) alot
tour tur
tourist information informasi turis
tourist turis
tow truck truk penarik
towel handuk
tower menara
town; town hall kota; balai kota
town square alun-alun
toy mainan
traces jejak
track (train) trek
traditional trdisional
traffic light lampu lalu lintas
trail lintasan
train kereta api
transfer v **(trains / flights)** transfer
translate v menerjemahkan
trash sampah
travel agency agen perjalanan
travel sickness mabuk perjalanan
traveler's check cek wisata
treat (to a drink) mentraktir
tree pohon
trim (hair cut) pangkas
trip perjalanan
trolley [BE] troli
trousers [BE] celana panjang
T-shirt kaos oblong

turn off (lights) padam
turn on (lights) menyala
TV TV
type v mengetik
tyre ban

U

ugly jelek
umbrella payung
unattended tidak ditunggui
unconscious tidak sadar
underground [BE] bawah tanah
underpants [BE] celana dalam
understand v mengerti / memahami
underwear pakaian dalam
unemployed tidak punya pekerjaan
United Kingdom United Kingdom Inggris
United States (U.S.) Amerika Serikat
university universitas
unleaded (gas) tidak bertimbal
unlimited tidak terbatas
upper sebelah atas
upset stomach sakit perut
urgent penting / mendesak
urine urin
use menggunakan

V

vacancy lowongan
vacation liburan
vaccination vaksinasi
vacuum cleaner penghisap debu
vagina vagina

vaginal infection infeksi vagina
valid berlaku
valley lembah
valuable berharga
value nilai
vegetable sayuran
vegetarian vegetarian
vehicle kendaraan
vehicle registration registrasi kendaraan
vending machine mesin vending
very sangat
viewpoint [BE] titik pandang
village kampung
visa visa
visit v mengunjungi
visiting hours jam kunjungan
visually impaired tidak bisa melihat jelas
vitamin vitamin
V-neck leher-V
volleyball game permainan bola voli
vomit muntah

W

wait v tunggu
waist pinggang
waiter pramusaji / pelayan
waiting room ruang tunggu
waitress pramusaji / pelayan
wake v bangun
wake-up call panggilan untuk bangun
walk v berjalan

wall clock jam dinding
wallet dompet
war memorial tugu peringatan
warm v (something); **warm** adj (temperature) menghangatkan v; hangat adj
wash v mencuci
washing machine mesin cuci
watch mengawasi / menonton
water skis ski air
waterfall air terjun
watermelon semangka
wear v memakai
weather cuaca
weave v menenun
week; week end seminggu; akhir pekan
weekly mingguan
welcome v selamat datang
well-rested istirahat
west barat
what apa
wheelchair; wheelchair ramp kursi roda; jalan kursi roda
when kapan
where di mana
white putih
who siapa
widowed janda
wife istri
window jendela
windsurfer selancar angin
wine list daftar minuman anggur
wireless internet service layanan

internet nirkabel
wireless phone telepon nirkabel
with dengan
withdraw *v* menarik
withdrawal (bank) penarikan
without tanpa
woman wanita
wool wol
work (function) bekerja
work *v*; **work** *n* bekerja *v*
  pekerjaan *n*
wrap bungkus
wrestling gulat
wrist pergelangan tangan
write menulis

Y

year tahun
yellow kuning
yes ya
yesterday kemarin
yoghurt yoghurt
you anda / kamu
you're welcome terima kasih kembali
young muda
your milik anda
youth hostel hostel kaum muda

Z

zoo kebun binatang
zucchini zukini

A

abu-abu gray
adik brother (younger)
adik perempuan sister (younger)
agen agency
agen perjalanan travel agency
ahli expert (skill level)
ahli mata optician
air bersoda sparkling water
air jeruk lemonade
air mancur fountain
air minum drinking water
air panas hot water
air terjun waterfall
akhir pekan week end
akomodasi accommodation
akses access
alamat address *n*
alasan excuse *n* / reason
alat pel mop
alat pemanas heater
alergi allergic
alergi akibat tanaman hay fever
alkohol alcohol
alot tough (food)
alun-alun town square
aman safe (protected)
ambil bagasi baggage claim
ambil koper baggage claim
ambulan ambulance
amplop envelope

anak child
anak laki boy
anak perempuan girl
anda you
aneh strange
anemia anemic
anestesi anesthesia *n*
anggur grape
angin badai thunderstorm
anjing dog
anjing pemandu guide dog
antibiotik antibiotic
anting earrings
antiseptik antiseptic
antre queue
apa what
apa kabar how are you
apa saja anything
apabila when
apartemen apartment
apel apple
api light *n* / fire
apotek chemist *[BE]*
arah direction
arang charcoal
area piknik picnic area
area untuk merokok smoking area
arena bermain arcade
arteri artery
artifisial artificial
asam sour

asin salty
asli authentic / real
asrama dormitory
asuransi insurance
asyik fun
aturan busana dress code
aula hall
aula konser concert hall
aula konvension convention hall
awal early
ayah father
ayam chicken
ayan epilepsy

B

babi pork
bagaimana how
bagasi baggage
bagus good
bahan fabric
bahasa language
bahasa Inggris English
bahaya danger
bahu shoulder
baik good / fine (greetings) / kind (person)
baju dress (piece of clothing)
baju renang swimsuit
bak cuci sink
balai kota city hall
balet ballet
ban tyre / tire
ban berjalan conveyor belt
bandara airport

bangun wake *v*
bantal pillow
bantuan assistance / help
bapak father / Mr / Sir
barang goods
barang dari alpaka pewter
barang tembikar pottery (goods)
barat west
baru new
basket basketball
baterai battery
batu giok jade
batuk cough
bawah tanah underground *[BE]*
bawang putih garlic
bayam spinach
bayi baby
bea-cukai customs
bebas free
bebas lemak fat free
bebas pajak duty-free
bebek duck (animal)
beberapa some
bekerja work (function) / work *v*
belajar learn *v* / study *v*
belanja shopping *v*
beli bebas over the counter (medication)
belimbing carambola (starfruit)
belum menikah single (unmarried)
bensin petrol *[BE]*
berangkat leave (depart) (planes) *v* / (buses, trains, etc.)
berani brave *adj*

berapa harganya how much (price)
beras rice
bercerai divorce v
berdansa dancing
berdarah bleed v
berenang swim v
berharga valuable
berhenti stop v
berikutnya next
berisi contain
berjalan walk v
berkemah camp v
berlaku valid
bermain play v
bernafas breathe v
berpisah separated (marriage)
bersepeda cycling
bersih clean adj
bertaruh bet v
bertemu meet (someone) v
bertunangan engaged (in a relationship)
besar big / large
besi iron n
besok tomorrow
BH bra
biasa regular (normal)
biaya fee / bill (charge) v / cost
bibir lip
bicara speak v
bioskop movie theater
bir beer
biru blue
bis bus

bisa can (yes) n
bisbol baseball
bisnis business
blus blouse
bohlam lightbulb
bokong buttocks
boks box
bon bill (money) n
boneka doll
botol bottle
botol bayi baby bottle
brokoli broccoli
bros brooch
buah-buahan fruits
buaian cot
buat janji appointment v
buatan artificial
bubur porridge
buka open
bukit hill
buku book n
buku panduan guide book
bulan month
bunga flower
bungkus wrap / take away (food) [BE]
buntut sapi oxtail
buruk sekali terrible
burung bird
busuk rotten

C

cacat disabled / handicapped
cagar alam nature preserve
candi temple (religious)

cangkir cup / mug v
cantik beautiful
cap stamp (a ticket) v
catatan notes [BE]
cek cheque [BE] / check n
cek wisata traveler's check
celana dalam briefs (clothing) /
  underpants [BE]
celana panjang pants / trousers [BE]
celana panjang ketat tights [BE]
celana pendek shorts
cemilan snacks
cenderamata souvenir
centimeter centimeter
cepat fast / quick
cerah sunny
cereal cereal
ceri cherry
cerutu cigar
cetak foto digital digital print
cincin ring
cinta love
cium kiss v
cod cod (type of fish)
cokelat brown / chocolates
contoh specimen
cuaca weather
cucu grandchild
cucu-cucu grandchildren
cukai duty (tax)
cumi squid

D

dada breast / chest (body part)

daftar barang itemize
daftar minuman anggur wine list
daging asin cured meat
danau lake
dansa dance v
dapat can (yes) n
**dapat dilalui penyandang
  cacat** handicapped-accessible /
  disabled accessible [BE]
dapur kitchen
darah blood
darmawisata sightseeing / excursion
darurat emergency
dasi tie (clothing)
datang come v / arrive v
datar flats (shoes)
daun leaf
daun bawang scallion [spring onion]
daur ulang recycling
dekat near / close adj
delima pomegranate
demam fever
denda fine (fee)
dengan with
deposito deposit (bank) n
derajat degrees (temperature)
deterjen detergent
di in
di balik tikungan around (the corner)
di belakang behind (direction)
di dalam inside
di dalam ruangan indoor
di luar outside
di mana where

di samping next to / next
di sana there
di seberang opposite
di sekitar nearby
di sini here
di sudut on the corner
diare diarrhea
dicuri stolen
digoreng fried (cooking method)
diizinkan menurut hukum
 Islam permissible according to Islamic
 law
dijinjing carry-on
dilarang prohibit v
dingin cold
dirampok robbed
direktori toko store directory
diskon discount
dokter anak pediatrician
dokter gigi dentist
dokter kandungan gynecologist
dolar dollar (U.S.)
domestik domestic
dompet wallet
dorong push v
dot bayi pacifier / soother [BE]
duduk sit v

E

efek samping side effect
ekses excess
ekspres express
ekstra extra
ekstra besar extra large (size)

ekstra kecil extra small (size)
emas gold
enak delicious
epilepsi epilepsy
ercis pea
es ice
eskalator escalator

F

faks fax n
faktur invoice
farmasi pharmacy
fasilitas facility
feri ferry
film movie / film (camera)
flu cold (sickness)
formula formula (baby)
formulir form (fill-in)
foto photo
foto digital digital photo
fotografi photography
fotokopi photocopy

G

gabung join v
gading tua beige
ganggang laut seaweed
gangguan pendengaran hearing
 impaired
ganti alter (clothing) v
gantungan kunci key ring
garasi garage
garpu fork
gas gas

gatal-gatal rash n
gedung building
gel gel (hair)
gelang bracelet
gelap dark
gelas glass (drinking)
gelas takaran measuring cup
gerai counter n
gerbang gate (airport)
gereja church
gigi tooth
gigi palsu denture
gigitan bites n
gigitan serangga insect bite
ginjal kidney (body part)
gratis free
grup group
gua cave
gula sugar
gulat wrestling
gunting scissors
gunting rambut haircut
gunung mountain
gurauan joke
gurita octopus

H

hadiah gift
hadir attend v
hai hi
haid menstruation / period (menstrual)
hairspray hairspray
hak sepatu tinggi high-heels
halal halal

halaman pages (in a book)
halo hello
ham ham (food)
hambar bland
hamil pregnant
handuk towel
handuk kertas paper towel
hangat warm (temperature) adj
hanya only
harap please
harga price / cost
hari day
hari ini today hari ini
hati liver (body part) / heart
haus thirsty
helm helmet
hewan animal
hiburan entertainment
hidangan pembuka appetizer
hidangan pendamping side dish
hidangan utama main course
hidung nose
hijau green
hilang lost
hitam black
hoki hockey
hostel kaum muda youth hostel
hubungan relationship
hujan rain n
hutan forest
hutan tadah hujan rainforest

I

ibu mother / Madam / Mrs

identifikasi identification (card)
ikan cucut swordfish
ikat pinggang belt
ilmiah science
imigrasi immigration
indah beautiful
infeksi infection
informasi information
informasi turis tourist information
Inggris British / United Kingdom United Kingdom
ini this
intan diamond
internasional international
istana palace
istirahat well-rested / break *v*
istri wife
itu that

J

jadwal schedule *n* / time table *[BE]*
jagung corn (vegetable)
jaket jacket
jaket pelampung life jacket
jalan road
jalan bebas hambatan highway
jalan kursi roda wheelchair ramp
jalan masuk entrance
jalan raya motorway (highway) *[BE]*
jalan satu arah one-way street
jalur line / path
jam hour / clock
jam alarm alarm clock
jam buka business hours

jam dinding wall clock
jam kerja office hours
jam kunjungan visiting hours
jamur mushroom
janda widowed
jangan diganggu do not disturb
jangka waktu period (of time)
jantung heart
jarang rare (object)
jari finger
jari kaki toe
jas coat / suit
jas hujan raincoat
jauh far
jejak traces
jelek ugly
jeli jelly (food)
jembatan bridge
jendela window
jeruk bali pomelo
jeruk keprok grapefruit
jeruk nipis lime
jingga orange (color)
jinjingan carry-on
jual sell *v*
juga too
jumlah amount / total
jurang cliff / ravine
jurusan stream (school)
jus juice

K

kabin cabin
kaca glass (material)

kacamata glasses (spectacles)
kacamata hitam sunglasses
kacang nuts (food)
kafe café
kain fabric
kakak brother (older)
kakak perempuan sister (elder)
kakek grandfather
kaki foot / leg
kali kecil stream
kalori calories
kalung necklace
kamar room
kamar kecil restroom (formal / informal)
kamar mandi bathroom
kambing lamb (meat)
kamera camera
kampung village
kamu you
kanan right (direction)
kangen missing (someone)
kantor office
kantor kurs mata uang currency exchange office
kantor polisi police station
kantor pos post office
kantung kemih bladder
kantung sampah garbage bag / rubbish bag [BE]
kantung tidur sleeping bag
kaos oblong T-shirt
kapal boat
kapan when

karton carton
kartu card
kartu isi top up card (phone value)
kartu keanggotaan membership card
kartu kredit credit card
kartu kunci key card
kartu memori memory card
kartu pos postcard
kartu telepon phone card
kasir cashier
kastil castle
kata sandi password
kathedral cathedral
Katolik Catholic
katun cotton
kaus kaki sock
ke dalam into
keamanan security
kebakaran fire
kebangsaan nationality
keberangkatan departure
kebun binatang zoo
kebun raya botanical garden
kecelakaan accident
kecil little / small
kecoa cockroach (bug)
kedatangan arrivals (airport)
kedelai soy bean
kehilangan missing (something) / lose v (something)
kejang cramps (menstruation)
kejang kalau haid menstrual cramp
keju cheese
kelas class

kelas bisnis business class
kelas ekonomi economy class
kelas satu first class
kelinci rabbit
kelompok group
keluar exit *v*
keluarga family
keluhan complaint
kemarin yesterday
kemasan package
kembalian change (money) *n*
kembang kol cauliflower
kemeja shirt
kendaraan vehicle
kentang potato
kepadatan congestion
kepiting crab (animal)
keputusan decision
kerang shellfish / clam
keranjang basket (grocery store)
kerapu carp (fish)
keras loud
kereta cart
kereta api train
kereta gantung cable car
kereta koper luggage cart
kertas paper
kertas WC toilet paper
kerusakan damage *n*
kesakitan pain
kesalahan mistake
kesehatan health
ketan gluten
ketat tight *adj*

khusus special
kilat express
kios koran newsstand
kipas fan (appliance)
kiri left (direction)
kirim send *v* / ship (mail) *v*
klub club
klub dansa dance club
klub malam nightclub
kocak funny
kode area area code
kode negara country code
koin coin
kol cabbage
kolam pond
kolam renang pool
kolam renang anak kiddie pool /
  paddling pool *[BE]*
kolega colleague
kompor gas stove
komputer computer
kondisi condition (medical)
kondom condom
koneksi connection (internet)
konferensi conference
konfirm confirm *v*
konser concert
konsulat consulate
konsultan consultant
kontak contact *v*
kontrol paspor passport control
konveyor conveyor belt
kopor luggage
kopor tangan hand luggage *[BE]*

koran newspaper
kosong empty
kostum costume
kota tua old town
kota town
kotak box
kotak pos postbox [BE]
kotak surat mailbox
kotor dirty
krim cream / ointment
krim cukur shaving cream
kualitas quality
kuku nail
kuku jari fingernail
kuku jari kaki toe nail
kulit leather / skin
kunci key / lock n
kunci kamar room key
kuning yellow
kurang less
kurma dates (fruit)
kurs exchange rate
kurs mata uang currency exchange
kursi chair
kursi dorong pushchair
kursi gantung chair lift (cable car)
kursi pantai deck chair
kursi roda wheelchair
kursi tinggi highchair
kwitansi bill (money) n

L

laci drawer
lagi again / more

lajang single (unmarried)
lalat fly (insect)
lama old (long ago)
lampu lamp
lampu lalu lintas traffic light
lantai floor
lantai dasar ground floor
lapangan court (sports) / field (sports)
lapangan golf golf course
lapar hungry
laporan polisi police report
lari run
laut sea
layanan internet internet service
layanan internet nirkabel wireless
   internet service
layanan lengkap full-service
lebih baik better
lebih besar bigger
lebih cepat faster
lebih kecil smaller
lebih lamban slower
lebih murah cheaper
lebih ringan lighter (less heavy)
leher neck
lelah exhausted / tired
lemari locker
lemari besi safe (object)
lemari es refrigerator
lemari kopor luggage locker
lemari pajangan display case
lembah valley
lembar sheet
lengan arm

lengan panjang long sleeves
lengan pendek short sleeves
lensa lens
lensa kontak contact lens
lezat delicious
liburan vacation / holiday *[BE]*
lidah tongue
lihat see *v*
lingkar leher baju crew neck
lintasan trail
lisensi licence
lokal local
loket ticket office
lorong aisle
loteng storey *[BE]*
lowongan vacancy
luar biasa magnificent
lucu funny
luka cut (injury) *n*
lurus straight / straight ahead
lusin dozen
lutut knee

M

maaf sorry / excuse me *v*
mabuk karena goyangan motion sickness
mabuk perjalanan travel sickness
macet jam (traffic) *n*
mahal expensive
mainan toy
majalah magazine
makan meal / eat *v*
makan malam dinner

makan pagi breakfast
makan siang lunch
makanan food
makanan bayi baby food
makanan cepat saji fast food
makanan kaleng canned goods
mal mall
mal perbelanjaan shopping mall
malam evening / night
malam ini tonight
malas lazy
maling break-in (burglary)
manajer manager
mangga mango
mangkuk bowl
manikur manicure
manis sweet (taste)
masakan dishes (food)
masalah problem
masukkan insert *v* (on an ATM)
mata eye
mata uang currency
matahari sun
medan perang battleground
meja table
meja informasi information desk / reservation desk
mekanis mechanic
melihat look
memahami understand *v*
memajang display *v*
memakai wear *v*
memanggang barbecue / bake *v*
memanggil call *v*

memangkas cut v (hair)
memasak cook v
memasuki enter v
mematikan log off
membaca read
membakar burn v
membalikkan reverse (the charges) [BE] v
membatalkan cancel v
membawa bring v
membayar pay v
membeli buy v
membengkak swelling
membereskan pack v
memberi makan feed v
memberi give v
memberitahu notify v
membersihkan clear v / clean v
membolehkan allow v
membosankan boring
memeriksa check v (something)
memerlukan need v
memesan book v / order v
memesan tempat reserve v
memiliki have v
memperbaiki mend v / repair v
memperkenalkan introduce v
mempunyai have v
memutar dial v
menagih charge (credit card) v
menaiki board v
menambah fill up v (food)
menambal filling (tooth)
menanggalkan take off (clothes) v

menara tower
menari dance v
menarik attractive / interesting / withdraw v
mencabut extract (tooth) v
mencapai reach v
mencengangkan stunning
mencetak print v
mencicip taste v
mencuci wash v
mencuri steal v
mendalam deeply
mendekat close v
mendesak urgent
menelepon phone v
menemui meet (someone) v
menerima accept v / receive v
menerjemahkan translate v
mengagumkan amazing
mengakhiri end v
mengambil pick up (something) / take (something) v
mengangu bother v
mengawasi watch
mengeluh complain
mengembalikan return (something) v
mengemudi drive v
mengepak pack v
mengerti understand v
mengetik type v
menggambar draw
menggunakan use
menghangatkan warm (something) v
menghapus delete v

mengisi fill out (form) *v*

mengisi ulang recharge *v*

mengizinkan permit *v*

mengosongkan empty *v*

mengubah change *v*

mengulang repeat *v*

mengunci lock up

mengunjungi visit *v*

menikah married / marry *v*

menikmati enjoy *v*

menit minute

menjadi be *v*

menjangkau reach *v*

menolak decline *v* (credit card)

menonton watch

mentah raw

mentega butter

mentraktir treat (to a drink)

menu harga pasti fixed-price menu

menu minuman drink menu

menukar exchange *v*

menular contagious

menulis write

menulis resep prescribe *v*

menunda delay *v*

menunjukkan show *v*

menutup close *v*

menyala turn on (lights)

menyalakan rokok light (cigarette) *v*

menyambung log on

menyatakan declare *v*

menyelam dive *v*

menyenangkan nice

menyerang attack (on person)

menyetor deposit *v*

menyewa rent *v*

menyukai like *v*

menyurati mail *v*

menyusui breastfeed

merah red

merah muda pink

merampok rob *v*

merekomendasi recommend *v*

merokok smoke *v*

merusak damage *v*

mesin cuci washing machine

mesin cuci otomatis laundromat

mesin cuci piring dishwasher

mesjid mosque

mie noodles

mil mileage

milik anda your

milik pria men's

minggu lalu last week

mingguan weekly

minum drink *v*

minuman beverage / drink *n*

minyak oil

minyak gosok cream / ointment

minyak wangi cologne

misa mass (church service)

mobil car

mobil otomatis automatic car

mobil sewa rental car / hired car

mobilitas mobility

mual nauseous

muda young

mudah easy

mulai begin *v* / start *v*
mulut mouth
mungil cute / petite
muntah vomit
murah cheap
musik klasik classical music
musik rakyat folk music
mutiara pearl

N

nadi artery
nama name
nanas pineapple
nangka jackfruit
nanti later
nenek grandmother
ngarai canyon / ravine
nilai value
nomor number
nomor identifikasi pribadi personal identification number (PIN)
nomor pesawat extension (phone)
nomor sim pengemudi driver's license number
nomor telepon phone number
Nona Miss
nyaring loud
nyata real
Nyonya Mrs / Madam

O

oatmeal oatmeal
obat medicine
obat penghilang sakit painkiller

obat tetes drop (medicine)
olahraga sports
ongkos fare (e.g taxi fare)
Orang America American (person)
Orang Australia Australian (person)
Orang China Chinese (person)
Orang Irlandia Irish (person)
Orang Kanada Canadian (person)
oranye orange (color)
orkestra orchestra
otot muscle

P

pabean customs
pacar boyfriend
padam turn off (lights)
pagi a.m. / morning
paha thigh
pajak bandara airport tax
pajak penjualan sales tax
pajangan display *n*
pakaian clothing
pakaian dalam underwear
paket package
palu hammer
panas heat / hot (temperature)
panci saucepan
panggang roast *v*
panggilan collect collect call
panggilan telepon phone call
panggilan untuk bangun wake-up call
pangkas trim (hair cut)
panjang long

pantai beach
papan seluncur surfboard
parkir park *v*
paruh waktu part-time
paru-paru lung
pas fit (clothing)
pasak tenda tent peg
pasar market
paspor passport
pasta gigi tooth paste
patah broken (bone)
patung statue
payung umbrella
pecah broken (glass)
pedas spicy / hot (spicy)
pedikur pedicure
pegang hold *v*
pejalan kaki pedestrian / stroller
pekerjaan work *n*
pelajar student
pelajar internasional international student
pelajaran lesson (learnt a lesson)
pelataran parkir parking lot
pelataran parkir mobil car park *[BE]*
pelayan waiter / waitress
pelayanan service (in a restaurant)
peluk hug *v*
pemandu guide (tourist) *n*
pemantik rokok lighter (cigarette)
pembalut wanita sanitary napkin / pad (for menstruation) *[BE]*
pembuka botol bottle opener
pembuka kaleng can opener

pemindai scanner
pemula beginner (skill level) / novice (skill level)
pena pen
penarikan withdrawal (bank)
penata rambut hairstylist
pencuri thief
pencurian theft
pendek short *adj*
penerbangan airline / flight
penerjemah lisan interpreter
pengacara lawyer
pengawasan supervision
pengembalian dana refund
pengering rambut hair dryer
pengetahuan knowledge
penggorengan frying pan
penggunaan eksternal external use
penghisap debu vacuum cleaner
pengukus steamer
pengusir serangga insect repellent
pening drowsiness
penis penis
penisilin penicillin
penjaga lifeguard
penjaga bayi babysitter
pensiun retired
penting urgent
penuh full
penumpang passenger
penyewaan mobil car rental
pepaya papaya (fruit)
per hari per day
per jam per hour

per malam per night
per minggu per week
perabotan rumah household goods
peradangan sendi arthritis
perahu motor motor boat
perahu penyelamat life boat
perak silver
perak murni sterling silver
perangko stamp (postage) *n*
perawat nurse
perbaiki fix (repair) *v*
perban bandage
perceraian divorce *n*
perempuan lady
pergelangan tangan wrist
pergi go (somewhere) *v*
pergi ke get to
perhiasan jewelry
periode period (of time)
periuk pot
periuk tembikar clay pot
perjalanan trip
perjalanan pulang-pergi round-trip
perjanjian appointment
perkebunan farm
perkemahan campsite
perkosa rape
perlahan-lahan slowly
perlengkapan equipment
perlengkapan menyelam diving
  equipment
perlengkapan olahraga sporting
  goods
permainan game

permainan bola voli volleyball game
permen candy / sweets *[BE]*
permen karet chewing gum
permisi excuse me *v*
peron platform
perpustakaan library
persendian joint (body part)
persimpangan intersection
pertama first
pertandingan match *n*
pertandingan tinju boxing match
pertanian farm
pertanyaan question
pertemuan meeting
perusahaan company (firm)
perusahaan asuransi insurance
  company
perut stomach
pesan message
pesan instan instant message
pesawat terbang airplane / plane
peta map *n*
peta jalan road map
pijat massage
pijat olahraga sports massage
pil pill (birth control)
pinggang waist
pintu door
pintu darurat emergency exit / fire
  door
pir pear
piring plate / dish (kitchen)
pisang banana
pisau knife

piyama pajamas

pohon tree

polisi police

pompa bensin gas station / petrol station

ponsel cell phone / mobile phone

popok diaper / nappy [BE]

porselen porcelain

porsi portion

porsi anak children's portion

pos post [BE]

pos udara airmail

pramusaji waiter / waitress

pria man

produk pembersih cleaning product

produk susu dairy

publik public

puing ruins

puncak peak (of a mountain)

punggung back (body part)

puri temple (religious)

pusat bisnis business center

pusat kaki lima hawker center

pusat kota downtown

pusat pertokoan department store

pusing dizzy / drowsiness

putih white

putri girl

putuskan hubungan disconnect (computer)

R

rabun dekat near-sighted / short-sighted [BE]

rabun jauh far-sighted (eye condition) / long-sighted [BE]

racun poison

radis radish

rahang jaw

ramalan forecast

rambut hair

ransel backpack

rapat meeting

ratu queen

rebus boil (cooking method)

rekan colleague

rekening account n

rekening giro checking account

rekening koran current account [BE]

rekomendasi recommendation

rem brakes (car)

rencana plan

rendah low

reruntuhan ruins

resep prescription

reservasi reservation

resi receipt

resor resort (holiday)

restoran restaurant

rias make up (face) v

rindu missing (someone)

ringan light (not heavy) adj

rok skirt

rokok cigarette

romantis romantic

roti bread

roti panggang toasted bread

ruang pas fitting room

ruang rapat meeting room
ruang tunggu waiting room
rumah home / house
rumah sakit hospital
rusak damaged / broken (machine) /
  break down *v*
rusuk rib (body part)
rute alternatif alternate route
rute sepeda bike route

S

sabun soap
sakit hurt / ill / sick
sakit dada chest pain
sakit jantung heart condition
sakit kepala headache
sakit perut stomachache / upset
  stomach
sakit telinga earache
sakit tenggorokan sore throat
saku pocket
salah mistake
salju snow *n*
salon rambut hair salon
sambung connect (internet) *v*
sambungan connection (internet)
sampah trash / rubbish
sandiwara play (theatre) *n*
sangat very
saos sauce
sapi beef
sapi jantan ox
sapu broom
sarapan breakfast

satpam security
satu one
Saudara Mr / Sir
Saudari Miss
sauna sauna
Saya I
sayuran vegetable
seafood seafood
sebelah atas upper
sebelah kanan right of way
sebelum before
sedih sad
segar fresh
seiris slice (of something)
sejuk cool (temperature)
sekali once
sekali jalan one-way (ticket)
sekali pakai disposable
sekarang now
sekolah school
sekuriti security
selada lettuce
selai jam (food)
selama during
selamat datang welcome *v*
selamat malam good evening
selamat pagi good morning
selamat siang good afternoon
selamat tinggal goodbye
selancar angin windsurfer
selatan south
seledri celery
selimut blanket
selop slippers

semalaman overnight
semangka watermelon
sembelit constipated
sementara temporary
seminggu week
senang pleased / happy / gay (happy)
sendal loafers / sandals
sendirian alone
sendok spoon
sendok keramik ceramic spoon
sengatan sting *n*
sengatan matahari sunburn / sunstroke
senter flashlight
sepak bola soccer / football game *[BE]*
separuh half
sepatu shoes
sepatu bot boots
sepatu kanvas sneaker
sepeda bicycle
sepeda motor motorcycle
sepotong piece
seprei sheet
serbet napkin
sereh lemongrass
sertifikat certificate
sesuatu anything
sesudah after
setelah after
setengah half
setrika iron (clothes) *v* / press (clothing) *v*
sewa hire *v [BE]*
sewa mobil car hire *[BE]*
sewaktu during

siang afternoon / p.m.
siap ready
siapa who
siapa saja anyone
sibuk busy
sikat rambut hairbrush
siku elbow
silakan please
simpan keep / save *v*
singkat short *adj*
sirop syrup
sisir comb
ski air water skis
soket listrik electric outlet
solar diesel
sore p.m.
sosis sausage
spesialis specialist (doctor)
stasiun station
stasiun bis bus station
stasiun kereta api railway station
stroberi strawberry
studi study *v*
suami husband
suara audio
sudut corner
suhu temperature
suka alergi allergic reaction
sulit difficult
sulit tidur insomnia
sumpit chopsticks
sungai river
sungai kecil stream
sungguh really

sup soup
supervisi supervision
surat letter / mail n
surat izin licence
surat kabar newspaper
surat tercatat registered mail
susu milk
susu kedelai soymilk
sutera silk
suvenir souvenir
swalayan self-service / supermarket

T

tabel konversi conversion table
tabir surya sunblock
tabrakan crash v (car)
tabungan savings (account)
tadi malam last night
tahan hold v
tahu bean curd / know
tahun year
tajam sharp
taksi taxi
taman park n
tanda tangan signature
tanda terima receipt
tangan hand
tangga stairs
tangga berjalan escalator
tanggal date (calendar)
tanpa without
tanpa alkohol non-alcoholic
tarian dancing
tarik pull v

tarik nafas panjang breathe deeply
tas bag
tas pakaian suitcase
tas tangan handbag [BE]
tata rambut hairstyle / style (hair)
tekanan darah blood pressure
teks text (send a message) v
teks film subtitle
telepon telephone / phone n
telepon bayar pay phone
telepon nirkabel wireless phone
teler hangover
telinga ear
telur egg
teman friend
teman perempuan girlfriend
tempat place n
tempat cukur barber
tempat duduk seat
tempat menarik attraction (place)
tempat tidur bed / berth
tempat tidur bayi crib / cot
tenang quiet
tenda tent
tendang kick
tengah hari noon / midday [BE]
tengah malam midnight
tenggorokan throat
tepat waktu on-time
terakhir last
terang light (bright) adj
terbaik best
terbang fly v
terburu-buru rush (in a rush)

terima kasih thank you
terima kasih kembali you're welcome
terinfeksi infected
terjal steep
terkilir sprain *v*
terlalu matang overdone
terlambat late (time)
termasuk include *v*
tiba arrive *v*
tidak no
tidak ada apa-apa nothing
tidak ditunggui unattended
tidak mahal inexpensive
tidak merokok non-smoking
tidak punya pekerjaan unemployed
tidak sadar unconscious
tidak tahan gula lactose intolerant
tidak terbatas unlimited
tidur sleep *v*
tikar mat (rug)
tiket ticket
tiket masuk admission (fees)
tiket masuk pesawat boarding pass
tiket pulang-pergi multiple-trip
  (ticket) / (return ticket) *[BE]* *n*
tikungan on the corner
tikus rat
tim team
timur east
tinggal stay *v* / live *v*
tinggi height / high
tingkat storey *[BE]*
tiram oyster
tisu tissue

titik pandang viewpoint *[BE]*
toko shop
tolong please
topi hat
toples jar
trek track (train)
troli trolley *[BE]* / luggage cart
truk penarik tow truck
tua old (person)
Tuan Mr / Sir
tujuan purpose
tukang daging butcher
tulang bone
tulang belakang spine (body part)
tulang iga spare ribs
tuli deaf
tumit ankle
tunda delay *n*
tunggu wait *v*
tur tour
tur darmawisata sightseeing tour
tur dengan bis bus tour
turis tourist
turun get off (a train / bus / subway)
tutup closed / close *adj*

U

uang money
uang muka cash advance
uang tunai cash *n*
uap steam *n*
udang shrimp
udara air
ukiran carvings *n*

ukuran size
ulang tahun birthday
umur age
unggas poultry
ungu purple
universitas university
untuk for
untuk dibawa to go
urin urine
usaha business
usia age
usus buntu appendix (body part)
utara north

W

wajah face
waktu time
wanita woman / lady
warga usia lanjut senior citizen
warna color
wilayah region
wol wool
wortel carrot

Z

zaitun olive
zukini zucchini